DATE DUE			

Annie Dillard

Twayne's United States Authors Series

Frank Day, Editor

Clemson University

TUSAS 588

ANNIE DILLARD
Photograph by John Montre.

Annie Dillard

By Linda L. Smith

University of Toledo

Twayne Publishers/New York
Maxwell Macmillan Canada/Toronto
Maxwell Macmillan International/
New York Oxford Singapore Sydney

Annie Dillard
Linda L. Smith

Copyright 1991 by G. K. Hall & Co.
All rights reserved.
Published by Twayne Publishers

Twayne Publishers
Macmillan Publishing Company
866 Third Avenue
New York, New York 10022

Maxwell Macmillan Canada, Inc.
1200 Eglinton Avenue East
Suite 200
Don Mills, Ontario M3C 3N1

Macmillan Publishing Company is part of the Maxwell Communication Group of Companies.

Copyediting supervised by India Koopman.
Book production by Janet Z. Reynolds.
Book design by Barbara Anderson.
Typeset by Graphic Sciences Corporation, Cedar Rapids, Iowa

10 9 8 7 6 5 4 3 2 1

Library of Congress Cataloging-in-Publication Data

Smith, Linda L.
    Anne Dillard / by Linda L. Smith.
        p.   cm. — (Twayne's United States authors ; TUSAS 588)
    Includes bibliographical references (p.   ) and index.
    ISBN 0-8057-7637-0
    1. Dillard, Annie—Criticism and interpretation.   I. Title.
II. Series.
PS3554.I398Z87   1991
818'.5409—dc20   91-14647

For Daddy

Contents

Preface

Annie Dillard stunned the literary world when at the remarkable age of 30 she won the 1975 Pulitzer Prize for general nonfiction. Her prizewinning book, *Pilgrim at Tinker Creek,* was hailed as a veritable masterpiece in the tradition of Thoreau's *Walden.* The success of *Pilgrim at Tinker Creek*—both in sales and in literary acclaim—is significant because it reflects important literary and social trends. Perhaps most important, it demonstrates a return to spiritual concerns in American literature, concerns rarely voiced since the nineteenth century's transcendental movement. In *Pilgrim at Tinker Creek* as in her other works, Dillard forcefully shows that an existential view of the human condition does not preclude a spiritual stance but instead demands it.

Dillard's work also demonstrates a renewed interest in the nonfiction essay, especially the blending of the essay with autobiography. She frequently uses incidents from her own life as springboards for discussing issues of more universal interest. Despite the autobiographical nature of her work, she has stated her willingness to sacrifice factual accuracy for the greater accomplishment of truth and art. This autobiographical approach reflects another twentieth-century preoccupation—the nature of human consciousness. As Dillard's career progresses, her work shows increasing interest in the creation of memory and its effect on self-identity, as well as the construction of perception itself.

Dillard's work reflects growing recognition of the necessity, in almost every arena of endeavor, of taking an interdisciplinary approach. Dillard herself fits the mold of the Renaissance "man"—she is knowledgeable in literature, art, philosophy, theology, natural science, history, and even quantum physics. Her every insight is filtered through and enriched by many layers of wisdom and knowledge. Such a background allows a broader, more integrated perspective on complex issues and increases awareness of the interconnectivity of all things and ideas.

While Dillard's work is at the forefront of modern thought and literature, she is also a firm respecter of tradition and culture. Her early love of the literary masters and her more recent interest in history reflect her recognition of the importance of a balance between the new and the old. She is not one of the recent breed of literary anarchists who seek originality at the expense of excellence, shunning tradition out of false principle. Rather, she wisely learns from tradition, retains what is excellent, and refashions it, making it her own.

All this is rightfully analytical and rational, but it ignores the emotional impact of Dillard's work, which is difficult to describe without rhapsodizing. She often emphasizes that she has a vision to convey, not a message—a critically important distinction. What an error it would be to mistake this book's analysis of her work for the vision that only the originals can bestow. Let it suffice to say that she deserves a reading.

This book discusses Dillard's major works from 1972 through 1989, in approximately chronological order. Chapter 1 is a brief biography, with heavy reliance on Dillard's memoir, *An American Childhood*. Chapters 2 through 7 provide a critical overview and analysis of the following works: *Pilgrim at Tinker Creek, Tickets for a Prayer Wheel, Holy the Firm, Teaching a Stone to Talk, Living by Fiction,* and *Encounters with Chinese Writers.* The conclusion assesses Dillard's career within the American literary tradition and points out common themes throughout her work, with an eye toward anticipating her future directions.

Acknowledgments

Before writing this, my first full-length book, I considered acknowledgments overly nice gestures of politeness. I now know that no exaggeration exists in the apparent overstatements of authors that "This book would not have been possible without the kind help of so-and-so, so-and-so, and so-and-so"—for in all sincerity, this book would not have been possible without the help of so many.

First, I must thank my doctoral committee chairman, Dr. Wallace Martin, who suggested the idea for this book and painstakingly read and commented on its hundreds of pages of manuscript, sometimes under unreasonable deadlines.

I also owe much to Dr. David Hoch and Dr. Robert Rudolph, who helped me obtain the graduate school fellowship supporting this endeavor and whose respect and encouragement have meant much to me for many years; the late Dr. Richard Summers, whose words of kindness throughout my graduate work helped keep me going; and Dr. Dorothy Siegel, whose interdisciplinary approach gave me new ideas about what could be achieved and how.

I cannot possibly express how greatly indebted I am to the work of Julie Parmenter, whose unpublished annotated bibliography of Annie Dillard's work saved me months, perhaps years, of effort. Nor can I adequately express my thanks to my husband, Richard, who read and edited every page, who kept me going when I was ready to give up, and who put up with my grumbling and complaints for months on end. I also thank my stepsons—Aaron, Adam, and Alex—for providing me with quiet when I needed to work and fun when I needed a break.

I thank all my wonderful friends, whose moral support I could not have done without, especially Nancy Simon, Lynn Anderson, Nancy Graumlich, and Sue Muller.

I also thank HarperCollins Publishers for permission to quote excerpts from *Pilgrim at Tinker Creek,* © 1974 by Annie Dillard, and the *Atlantic Monthly* for permission to quote excerpts from "Metaphysical Model with Feathers," © 1978.

Chronology

1945   Meta Ann Doak born on 30 April in Pittsburgh, Pennsylvania.

1955   Enters Ellis School in Pittsburgh.

1963   Enters Hollins College in Roanoke, Virginia.

1965   Marries R. H. W. Dillard on 5 June.

1966   "Overlooking Glastonbury" and "The Affluent Beatnik" (poems). Phi Beta Kappa.

1967   Completes B.A. in English literature, Hollins.

1968   Completes M.A. in English literature, Hollins.

1972   "Life Class" (fiction).

1973   "Monster in a Mason Jar," "Heaven and Earth in Jest," and "The Force That Drives the Flower" (essays).

1974   *Tickets for a Prayer Wheel* (poetry) and *Pilgrim at Tinker Creek* (prose narrative).

1975   Divorced from R. H. W. Dillard. On 5 May receives Pulitzer Prize for general nonfiction, and on 16 November receives Front Page Award for Excellence from New York Newswomen's Club for "Innocence in the Galapagos" (essay). Moves to island in Puget Sound, Washington, and becomes scholar-in-residence at Western Washington University in Bellingham.

1977   *Holy the Firm* (prose narrative).

1978   "The Living" (short story).

1979   Visiting professor at Wesleyan University in Middletown, Connecticut.

1980   Marries Gary Clevidence on 12 April.

1981   Scholar-in-residence, Western Washington University.

1982   *Teaching a Stone to Talk* (essays) and *Living by Fiction* (criticism). Visits China in May and June as part of State Department cultural delegation. Attends U.S.–China Writers Conference, UCLA.

1983   Returns to Wesleyan. Phi Beta Kappa orator, Harvard/Radcliffe commencement exercises.

1984   *Encounters with Chinese Writers* (prose narrative). Birth of daughter, Cody Rose.

1985   Receives John Simon Guggenheim Foundation grant.

1987   *An American Childhood* (memoir).

1988   Divorced from Gary Clevidence. Marries Robert D. Richardson, Jr.

1989   *The Writing Life* (prose narrative). Writer-in-residence, Wesleyan University.

Annie Dillard

Twayne's United States Authors Series

Frank Day, Editor

Clemson University

TUSAS 588

Chapter One

Country Clubs, Girls' Schools, and That Kind of Stuff

"I never expected to see a manuscript this good in my life. . . . The chance to publish a book like this is what publishers are here for."[1] This was the response of editor in chief Larry Freundlich of Harper's Magazine Press, which published Annie Dillard's Pulitzer Prize–winner, *Pilgrim at Tinker Creek,* in March 1974. It was only one of many accolades she would receive for her account of a year spent with nature in the Roanoke Valley. *Pilgrim at Tinker Creek* has more than fulfilled Freundlich's expectations. Critics compared it favorably with *Walden* and labeled Dillard a modern-day Thoreau. By 1987 it had sold 55,000 copies in hardback and more than 600,000 in paperback, and it has been reprinted in London, Amsterdam, Stockholm, São Paulo, and Tokyo. The accomplishment is all the more remarkable because Dillard was only 29 when she completed the book.

In the years following *Pilgrim at Tinker Creek,* Dillard has continued to surprise readers and critics alike with her ongoing originality, her ever-fresh wit, her lively storytelling, and her awe-inspiring sense of the numinous. While Dillard has called herself a Christian mystic whose audience is primarily agnostic nonbelievers, she considers herself an artist rather than a theologian or exegete. As she has expressed it, she seeks to convey a vision, rather than a message, and her main concern is the artistic structure of her work. As a result of her success at accomplishing her aesthetic concerns, her work is read and appreciated by both those whose interest is literature and those whose interest is spirituality. In fact, she has become an acknowledged authority on the writing of the narrative essay, and excerpts of her work are included in dozens of freshman composition anthologies.

In addition to *Pilgrim at Tinker Creek,* Dillard has produced seven books, which include a volume of poems, *Tickets for a Prayer Wheel; Holy the Firm,* a lyric, three-part narrative examining human suffering; *Teaching a Stone to Talk,* a book of essays covering a variety of topics; *Living by Fiction,* a work of literary criticism that also contains philosophical musings on the nature of meaning; and *Encounters with Chinese Writers,* an account of Dillard's experiences as part of a cultural delegation to China in 1982. Her most recent works include the memoir *An American Childhood* and a book describing the inner life of a writer, *The Writing Life*. In addition, Dillard has published a number of miscellaneous essays and poems. While nonfiction is her forte, she has long expressed an interest in fiction as well and has published about a dozen short stories, the most notable of which is "The Living" (1978), about a man whose life is miraculously transformed when he receives a death threat.[2]

It is tempting to call Annie Dillard an enigma. More than one journalist has emphasized the apparent incongruity between Dillard the person and the visionary persona that appears in her work. Even those who know her are sometimes astonished that this down-to-earth person they know so well could produce such soaring, often-ethereal prose. Dillard herself recalls a friend, a theology student at Yale, who was amazed anew after reading *Holy the Firm* that her "pen pal" Annie could also be a prophet and a saint.[3] Literary critics, trained to distinguish between author and persona, have somewhat less trouble in this regard. Still, Dillard's use of the first person and her frequent culling of her personal experiences for her writing make it sometimes difficult to keep the distinction in mind. Dillard, of course, sees no contradiction between her life and her work, and she is quick to point out that she is indeed no saint. "I don't know anything about God, any more than anybody else does," she proclaims. "I do not live well. I merely point to the vision."[4]

Despite such disclaimers, Dillard is still pursued by seekers who believe she can convey to them, to use a hackneyed phrase, the purpose of life and the meaning of the universe. In a 1983 interview, for instance, she stated that strangers regularly arrive at her home unannounced, like pilgrims to a shrine. And in 1987, almost fifteen years after the publication of *Pilgrim at Tinker Creek,* she said that a day does not pass without the arrival of a letter from someone who has recently read the book. "They feel like they have each discovered me individually," she explained.[5] She is clearly somewhat dismayed by the volume of mail she receives and the burden of disenchanting those who are overly idealistic. But she cannot hide her pleasure at those whose lives seem to have been truly changed by reading her books: "I never suspected when I started writing that people's lives were going to be changed. Not in a million, trillion, billion, billion years. But there is some guy that quit teaching theology at Loyola because of *Pilgrim*. And he decided after reading *Pilgrim* that intellect had done all it could, and for ultimate final questions you had to turn to art" (Burnett, 89).

Perhaps in the final assessment, Dillard is no more an enigma than anyone else is. In many ways she embodies the contradictions she sees at work in the world and in the human psyche. In one of the essays in *Teaching a Stone to Talk,* "An Expedition to the Pole," she proclaims that wherever human-kind may go in its explorations, "there seems to be only one business at hand—that of finding workable compromises between the sublimity of our ideas and the absurdity of the fact of us."[6] Dillard is undoubtedly humble enough to include herself in that statement. The following look at her life investigates the forces that helped create the sublimity and absurdity in her own richly complex personality.

The Childhood Years

Annie Dillard was born Meta Ann Doak on 30 April 1945 in Pitts-burgh, Pennsylvania. She was the oldest of Frank and Pam Doak's three daughters; her sister Amy was born when she was 3 and Molly was born when she was 10. Dillard's parents were well-to-do, and their children were brought up in affluent circumstances. In a 1977 interview, with a tone of rebellious disdain Dillard described growing up in a world of "country clubs, girls' schools, that kind of thing," but she also stressed that she had a happy childhood.[7]

As Dillard describes them in *An American Childhood,* her parents were idiosyncratic, to say the least. Unwittingly, they raised her in the way that psychologists now know produces creative, often-gifted children. She was given great freedom and encouraged to make her own decisions, take risks, and be a nonconformist. Her parents' emphasis on jokes and storytelling helped further develop her creative talents. "Remembering jokes was a moral obligation," she explains in her memoir.[8] She describes how the fam-ily would discuss the delivery of a single joke for hours, experimenting with voice intonation, gestures, and wording until it was perfected. Practical jokes were also much encouraged in her home. Dillard awoke one Christmas morning, for instance, to find—what else?—a plastic manikin's leg in her stocking. The result of these early experiences frequently shows up in Dillard's light, dry humor and her superb storytelling ability.

Dillard's mother, Pam (Lambert) Doak, embodied some of the same contradictions that appear in her daughter. As Dillard describes her mother, she was wickedly witty, irreverent, nonconformist to an extreme, vigorously energetic, an amateur inventor, and an inveterate player of practical jokes. Pam Doak was also capable of being tenderly affectionate, nostalgic, and traditionally proper. She insisted that her children develop their own opin-ions, and she was not above ridiculing them for following the crowd. She was also a great social liberal, eschewing racial bigotry and defending the poor. One of Dillard's earliest memories is the lecture she received from her mother when, as a child of five, she innocently addressed the family's black maid using a racial slur she had learned from another child. Dillard's memoir of her childhood would be worth reading if it contained nothing except her fascinating portrayal of this remarkable woman.

Dillard's father, Frank Doak, was another original character. A Pittsburgh executive in the family business, American Standard Corporation, he quit his corporate job when Dillard was 10 to journey down the Mississippi River in his 24-foot cabin cruiser. His goal was to relive Mark Twain's *Life on the Mississippi,* his favorite book, and to visit New Orleans, the birthplace of Dixieland jazz. After six weeks he got lonely, sold the boat, and flew home, having traveled no farther than Louisville, Kentucky. When he returned to Pittsburgh, he became business manager of a recording studio. Another of Frank Doak's favorite books was Jack Kerouac's *On the Road,* which he and his daughter read and reread and frequently discussed. From her father Dillard learned much about how things work in the world. From plumbing to the world economic system, he was the authority—or at least he appeared so until Dillard realized, as all children someday do, that her father was sometimes wrong.

Her father's parents also played a large part in Dillard's life. Her grandparents lived in Pittsburgh most of her childhood, and she and her sister Amy spent much time with them. Dillard was named after her grandmother, Meta Waltenburger Doak, whom she describes in her memoir as "an imperious and kindhearted grande dame of execrable taste, a tall, potbellied redhead, a proud descendant and heir of well-to-do Germans in Louisville, Kentucky" (*AAC,* 49). In 1848 Meta Doak's grandfather had founded American Standard Corporation in Louisville, and the family still had holdings in the firm during Dillard's childhood.

Dillard's grandfather, Frank Doak, Sr., fit the perfect image of a grandfather—kind, good-natured, and tolerant of children. Originally from Pittsburgh, he was a banker and looked the part. He smoked cigars and wore vests complete with the obligatory pocket watch. His death from a brain tumor when Dillard was 13 was one of her earliest personal losses. Soon after his death, Dillard's grandmother moved to Florida, and Dillard's family bought and moved into her grandparents' house. Along with her sister Amy, Dillard visited her grandmother in Florida on spring vacations until she was 16, when jobs and other activities began to interfere with making the trip.

As a child Dillard collected insects and rocks, played detective, learned the Morse code, took drawing and piano lessons, attended dancing school, and collected pond water for microscope examination—just for starters. She played baseball or softball whenever she could. She also read continually. In her memoir she tells of discovering at the Homewood Library in Pittsburgh *The Field Book of Ponds and Streams,* which she considered a treasure trove of information about the natural world; she reread it year after year. While she enjoyed many books about the natural sciences, she learned early to be cautious of fiction, which she found ranged dramatically in quality.

When Dillard was 10 her parents enrolled her in a private school for girls, the Ellis School, from which she graduated in 1963. At the Ellis School she was exposed to a number of highly educated, well-mannered European teachers who had fled Europe during Hitler's rise to power. This influence, along with her reading of the many war novels of the 1950s, made her aware of the tenuousness of life and the fragility of happiness. The cold war, with its air-raid drills and talk of nuclear war, added to her anxiety and left her—like many children of the period—worried about how well her family might survive in the event of war, forced to live only on the food stored in their basement.

The High School Years

When Dillard was 14, she began a journal collection of her favorite poetry. It included bits by Edna St. Vincent Millay, Rupert Brooke, Wilfred Owen, T. S. Eliot, Arthur Rimbaud, Paul Verlaine, and others, as well as much haiku and some of her favorites translated from other languages, such as Greek and Sanskrit. She began writing poetry herself, sometimes in French or German, which she was studying, along with Latin, at the Ellis School. She often wrote poems imitating her favorite poet, the French symbolist Rimbaud.

By this time Dillard had developed a firm religious background. Throughout her childhood, her parents had forced her and her sister Amy to attend the Shadyside Presbyterian Church, although her parents did not attend themselves. Dillard also attended a fundamentalist church camp in the country for four consecutive summers. In *An American Childhood* she states that she "had got religion" at the church camp, and prayed each night at home for a grateful heart—which she reports she quickly lost because in her adolescent rebellion she hated everyone. At church camp, at Sunday school, and at the Ellis School, Dillard had to memorize a great many Bible passages. She incorporated them into her poetry experiments, writing poems imitating the style of the Psalms and the Song of Songs.

In her memoir Dillard describes her experiences at dancing school learning ballroom dances, and later at the country-club subscription dances she and her dancing-school friends were invited to. While she greatly enjoyed the romantic atmosphere of the dances and her first interaction with boys in a formal social setting, this was also the beginning of her exposure to the affluent society of Pittsburgh that she would eventually grow to despise.

In high school Dillard sneaked cigarettes, drank coffee, played the guitar, and wore black turtleneck sweaters. Gradually she grew into an angry, rebellious teenager. She later described herself—accurately, it appears—as "wild in high school."[9] In her memoir she illustrates the increasing intensity of her life with the metaphor of the games of lightning chess that she and her boyfriend played—10 games per hour. When she was 16, she got into an accident while drag racing, ended up on crutches, and had to appear in juvenile court. She was also suspended from school for smoking. While her parents tried to decide what to do with her, she buried herself ever more deeply in poetry. Complaining about the hypocrisy, she also quit the church in rebellion; however, within the month she was apparently lured back by the writings of C. S. Lewis, loaned to her by her minister when she announced her intention to quit.

As almost all teenagers do, Dillard somehow survived her painful high school years. Perhaps it was her spiritual beliefs that saved her, or her growing interest in the transcendental views of Ralph Waldo Emerson. Or maybe it was the kind visits of her sister Amy to her bedroom when she was grounded, or the companionship of her like-minded boyfriend, Ralph. In any event, in Dillard's senior year the headmistress of the Ellis School, Marion Hamilton, recommended that Dillard attend Hollins College, her own alma mater and the place she sent all her "problem students." To Dillard's parents it sounded like a good idea. And so it was decided.

The College Years

At Hollins College, located near Roanoke in southwestern Virginia, Dillard enrolled in the creative writing program. She also took courses in theology, which attracted her, she once explained, "because of the beauty of it" (Moritz, 112). Apparently the environment at Hollins suited her, as her parents had hoped, for she did very well in her courses. She did so well, in fact, that she was granted membership in Phi Beta Kappa in 1966, her junior year of college.

At the end of her sophomore year, on 5 June 1965, Dillard married her creative writing teacher, Professor Richard Henry Wilde Dillard. He was nine years her senior and himself a poet, critic, novelist, and specialist in horror films. Richard Dillard greatly influenced his wife's writing, especially her poetry, during the 10 years of their marriage. Years after their divorce she still admitted humbly that he "taught me everything I know" (Lindsey, 7). One technique she learned from him was beginning a poem with a quotation by another writer or other authority—a technique she also carried into her prose works. Other obvious similarities can be seen in their writing, such as a common interest in natural history, a concern with the fall of man into time, and the use of common imagery, such as Eskimos and arches. Richard Dillard's literary associations probably also helped Annie get her work published. In 1966, for example, two of her early poems, "Overlooking Glastonbury" and "The Affluent Beatnik," appeared in publications edited by his friend and colleague at Hollins, George Garrett.[10]

Annie Dillard herself frequently shows up in the poetry Richard Dillard wrote during their marriage. It provides some of the few personal views of her that are on public record, outside her own writing and interviews. One of these poems, "Hats,"[11] presents a whimsical view of Annie modeling an entire stack of hats for her husband and his friends. It ends with a tender statement of his appreciation of her loveliness and gentleness. Another, "Annie Sleeping," is a poignant description of her peacefulness while sleeping, a peacefulness so intense and palpable that it renews her watching husband's faith that the pains of this life can be somehow, somewhere, transcended.[12] Other poems by Richard Dillard describe their home, their wedding trip, their anniversary, and other aspects of their life together. These poems hint at the intensity between these two writers whose poetic sensibilities and creative temperaments must have clashed at times.

After marrying, Dillard continued her college education, graduating in 1967 with her bachelor's degree in English literature. The following year she received her master's degree, writing a 40-page thesis entitled "Walden Pond and Thoreau." Her thesis discusses Walden Pond as the central image in *Walden* and the focal point for Thoreau's narrative movement between heaven and earth. Dillard spent the next year painting because, as she explains it, she felt she had been given a talent by God and had a duty to develop it; looking back later, she called the year "wasted."[13] She continued her reading as well as her writing of poetry, having a number of poems accepted for publication in such journals and magazines as *Southern Poetry Review, American Scholar,* and the *Atlantic.* She also took part in a number of volunteer activities, including working for Total Action against Poverty and reading for the blind at a local college.

The Tinker Creek Years

When Dillard describes the years between her graduation and the beginning of her work on *Pilgrim at Tinker Creek,* she sounds almost guilty that
they were not what society would consider productive. As she remarked to
one interviewer, "essentially my life was devoted to pinochle and badmin-
ton, ping-pong and reading," but she says she continually reminded herself
that "dammit, you've got to do something with your life" (Burnett, 91). In
retrospect, her decision to write a book appears to have resulted from a coincidence of events. To begin with, in 1970 she quit smoking and, needing
something to do with her hands, began a journal in a spiral notebook. She
quickly became completely devoted to her journals, writing down observations of the natural world, interesting quotations, theological speculations,
and other odd bits of information. Since she lived near Tinker Creek at the
time, many of her journal entries described her experiences in the area
around it.

In 1971 Dillard had a near-fatal bout with pneumonia that indirectly
also contributed to the writing of *Pilgrim at Tinker Creek.* Her recovery
from this illness left her determined to experience life more fully—that is,
life outside the literary ivory tower. As a result, she began a series of camping trips, often alone, that provided even more fertile observations and speculations for her journals. On one of these, reading as always, she finished a
particularly bad book and, in a moment of defiance, decided to write one
herself. By the time she began her book, her journals had swelled to 20 volumes, and she began to transfer them onto four-by-six index cards, with an
elaborate system of cross-indexing. It was from 1,100 of these cards that
Dillard fashioned the text of *Pilgrim at Tinker Creek.*

Pilgrim at Tinker Creek describes the four seasons Dillard spent at Tinker
Creek in 1972; however, she did most of the actual writing of the book the
following year. She wrote the first half at home during the spring of 1973
and the remainder that summer at a study carrel in the Hollins College library, working a total of about eight months. She reports that when she
began the project she wrote only one or two hours a day. In the last two
months, however, as she neared completion of the book, she increased her
pace, some days writing as many as 15 or 16 hours.

In *The Writing Life* Dillard describes these months of writing *Pilgrim at
Tinker Creek.* She was so absorbed in her writing that she cut herself off
from society entirely. She quit going to the movies, watching television, attending parties and other social activities, and finally even reading the
newspaper—an activity she dearly loved. She subsisted on coffee and Coca-

Cola, lost 30 pounds, and let all her plants die from lack of care. When she found herself being distracted by the view outside her carrel window, she closed the blinds for good and taped to their closed slats a drawing she had earlier made of the view. In *The Writing Life* she tells of opening the slats a bit one night and being stunned to see the sky filled with fireworks: she had forgotten it was the Fourth of July.

When Dillard had completed only two chapters of *Pilgrim at Tinker Creek,* she decided to see whether she could get them published. Her husband's agent, Blanche Gregory, agreed to be her agent but nixed Dillard's idea of submitting the manuscript under a man's name. Dillard explained later that she had considered the deception because she couldn't think of a single book about theology written by a woman other than Simone Weil.[14] That issue settled, Gregory immediately submitted one chapter to the *Atlantic* and another to *Harper's.* Both were quickly accepted. "Monster in a Mason Jar," which became chapter 3 in the book, appeared in *Harper's* in the August issue. *Harper's* also published another chapter, "Heaven and Earth in Jest," in its October issue; under the same title, that segment later appeared as the first chapter of the book. In October Dillard finally completed *Pilgrim at Tinker Creek.* The next month, in November, "The Force That Drives the Flower" appeared in the *Atlantic;* that segment appeared as chapter 10 in the book.

By this time everything was happening very quickly. Lawrence Freundlich, editor in chief of Harper's Magazine Press, had seen the excerpts from *Pilgrim at Tinker Creek* and offered Dillard a contract for the entire book. Dillard accepted the contract after Gregory insisted that Freundlich promise to give the book special care in publishing and marketing. By this time *Harper's* had also invited Dillard to become a contributing editor, a position she held off and on through the 1980s. She also served as a columnist from 1973 to 1975 for *Living Wilderness* magazine, the periodical of the Wilderness Society, writing essays that appeared in a column entitled "Sojourner."

During this period Dillard had also negotiated a contract with the University of Missouri Press to publish a book of her poetry. That volume, *Tickets for a Prayer Wheel,* was released early in 1974, only a few months before the publication of *Pilgrim at Tinker Creek. Tickets for a Prayer Wheel* contained 24 of Dillard's poems, many of which had appeared previously in journals and magazines. It received moderate attention, with a handful of favorable reviews, and demonstrated some promise for Dillard's skill as a poet. Its time in the limelight was cut short, however, by the publication of *Pilgrim at Tinker Creek* in March 1974.

From the start, *Pilgrim at Tinker Creek* was an acknowledged winner. The appearance of excerpts from the book in *Harper's* and the *Atlantic* had the critics' appetites whetted well in advance of its release. Consequently, when it came out in its entirety, they pounced on it with relish. The acceptance of *Pilgrim at Tinker Creek* as the Book-of-the-Month Club's April selection further ensured that all reasonably attentive members of the literary world knew of its arrival. Most of the reviews—which appeared by the dozens—were enthusiastically favorable, with only a few voicing the complaint about Dillard's overwriting that would follow much of her career. A few reviewers also had difficulty accepting the spiritual overtones in *Pilgrim at Tinker Creek*. Yet despite these isolated grumblings, Dillard was now a celebrity in the literary world, if not in the eyes of the general public. She began to receive requests to make appearances and to undertake special writing projects.

During this whirlwind, Dillard's marriage of nine years to R. H. W. Dillard was breaking up. The couple separated shortly after the publication of *Pilgrim at Tinker Creek* in 1974 and divorced in 1975. Dillard has never publicly discussed the reasons for the divorce, not even to state whether the decision was mutual or the choice of only one of the parties. She has denied, however, that the divorce had anything to do with her writing success. Regardless of the reasons for the divorce, it was undoubtedly a grievous experience for Dillard and probably played a large part in her growing sense of the inevitability of loss—a theme that appears increasingly in her writing henceforth.

On 5 May 1975, 13 months after the publication of *Pilgrim at Tinker Creek,* Dillard was awarded the Pulitzer Prize for general nonfiction. Receipt of this honor, more than any other event, marked her achievement of true celebrity status and irrevocably changed her life. Dillard quickly found herself feeling like a commodity of which everyone wanted a share. She was inundated by requests—to write books, Hollywood scripts, words for songs, and even ballets; to speak and to teach; and to appear on television programs, including Johnny Carson's "Tonight Show." In addition, she began to find herself at the receiving end of piles of personal letters from readers who sought her advice and solace. Shortly after receiving the Pulitzer Prize, Dillard received—on 16 November 1975—the Front Page Award for Excellence from the New York Newswomen's Club for her article "Innocence in the Galapagos," published in the May issue of *Harper's*. But rather than pleasing Dillard, receipt of this additional award almost spooked her, making her feel even more isolated by her fame.

Dillard later admitted that she was frightened and confused by her rapid rise to celebrity status and the loss of privacy that accompanied it. In a 1977 interview she still appeared troubled, perhaps even guilty, about her success, which she considered "absolutely random." It disturbed her that many excellent writers had never received recognition for their work. She also seemed annoyed that she had been "marketed" as a somewhat mysterious, attractive young recluse. She commented cynically, "You feel maybe your success is partly because you have yellow hair and beautiful legs." Dillard was also resentful that certain publications that had earlier rejected her poetry wrote to her after she became famous, asking for something of hers to print. With more than a little bitterness she told the interviewer that she often sent them the same work they had previously rejected. She felt they wanted to cash in on her name now that she was famous. "It's a crooked business," she complained (Lindsey, 7).

Dillard was also repelled by the materialism of the New York literary world. It seemed to her that most of the literary people she met in New York City were more interested in talking about their investments than in discussing literature. Her opinion has not improved with the passage of time. In 1988, when working on *The Writing Life,* she told an interviewer that she was including in the book some passages about her negative experiences in New York immediately after the success of *Pilgrim at Tinker Creek.* She stated that she saw New York as "hell," and that "I came to New York and thought, 'These people are savages. They thought they were civilization.'" [15] Although these judgments did not make it into the final version of *The Writing Life,* they help illustrate Dillard's state of mind in the years following the publication of *Pilgrim at Tinker Creek.*

The Washington Years

The circumstances surrounding the success of *Pilgrim at Tinker Creek* helped Dillard make the decision to resist what she saw as the corrupting influence of fame. Rather than become a hack turning out easy-to-write bestsellers, she decided to move to the Pacific Northwest and rededicate herself to the art of writing. She accepted a position as scholar-in-residence at Western Washington University in Bellingham, Washington, a position she retained from 1975 to 1979 and again in 1981. She at first taught poetry but later switched to teaching prose writing. About this time she stopped writing poetry herself, feeling that her poetry was "no good" and that prose could do everything poetry can and more (Trueheart, 2).

When Dillard first moved to Washington, in 1975, she lived in a one-room log cabin on an isolated island in Puget Sound. She reports that she was "not very grown up; . . . I was a sheltered innocent" who was terribly lonely (Lindsey, 7). She felt that all her life she had been under the protection of a man, first her father and then her husband, and now she was truly on her own for the first time. Shortly after her move, she began work on *Holy the Firm,* in which she struggled with the themes she was facing in her life—sacrifice, loneliness, and dedication to art.

Dillard has stated that *Holy the Firm,* which remains her favorite of all her books, was the most difficult to write. Although its completed handwritten manuscript was a scant 43 pages, it took 15 months to write. She completed it in the winter of 1977, and it was published that fall. It received favorable reviews, but its theological and philosophical complexity made it less appealing to general readers than *Pilgrim at Tinker Creek.* Despite its inaccessibility, *Holy the Firm* reaffirmed Dillard's dedication to art and her rejection of the superficiality of celebrity.

Within a year of moving to Washington, Dillard met Gary Clevidence, a novelist and anthropology professor at Fairhaven College. The two lived together for several years and married on 12 April 1980. Clevidence's interest in fiction must have spurred Dillard to write more fiction, for during her years in Washington she wrote a number of short stories, including "The Living," which she considers one of her more important works and which was published in *Harper's* in November 1978. In 1977 she received the Washington Governor's Award for Literature.

The Connecticut Years

In 1979 Dillard accepted a position as Distinguished Visiting Professor at Wesleyan University in Middletown, Connecticut. In 1981 she returned to Western Washington University with her husband; they remained there until 1983, when the couple separated and she returned to Wesleyan to teach poetry and creative writing. In 1982 she published a book of her selected essays, *Teaching a Stone to Talk,* which received excellent reviews. That year she also published *Living by Fiction,* a book of literary theory; it received favorable but not rave reviews.

In May and June 1982 Dillard was part of a State Department cultural delegation to China comprised of scholars, publishers, and writers. In September she helped host a Chinese-American writers' conference in Los Angeles and accompanied the Chinese delegation on some of their travels in this country. She later received a grant from the National Endowment for the Arts to write her account of these experiences, *Encounters with Chinese Writers,* published in 1984. That book, which shows the sometimes-humorous, sometimes-profound nature of human interaction, was not widely reviewed, but it was generally well received.

In the summer of 1984 Dillard's relationship with Gary Clevidence resulted in the birth of her daughter, Cody Rose. Shortly afterward Dillard began thinking and writing about her own formative years. The result was *An American Childhood,* Dillard's memoirs of her childhood and youth, a book written with the aid of a John Simon Guggenheim Foundation grant and published in 1987. Dillard's sense of propriety showed itself in her treatment of friends and family members in *An American Childhood.* She refused to comply with her editor's and agent's requests to add more of her love life to the book; her response was that she didn't want "to kiss and tell" because "it's not ladylike" (Trueheart, 3). She also told her parents she would cut from the book anything they found objectionable, and she in fact did remove a few things at their request.

Dillard's original vision of *An American Childhood* was that it would "encompass the whole sweep of American history."[16] As early as 1981 she expressed a growing interest in history, and in 1987 she summed it up as follows: "First you're just a little blur, and then you gradually notice you're a person and then as you grow morally you notice you're a person in history and what you do matters, historically" (Trueheart, 2). In *An American Childhood* this view originally took the form of chapters, interspersed throughout the book, describing the history of the Pittsburgh area—the arrival of the Scottish-Irish in Pittsburgh, the French and Indian Wars and the War of 1812, the early days of steel making, and so forth. Both Dillard's agent and her friend and biographer Phyllis Rose, however, urgently recommended omitting most of these chapters. According to Dillard, Rose likened their effect to the voice of John Cameron Swayze interrupting what was otherwise a masterpiece (Trueheart, 2). Even worse, Dillard's agent actually removed the offending chapters, without Dillard's authority, before submitting the book to Harper and Row. Dillard was so shocked that she compliantly acquiesced to the removal of the chapters.

Despite the deletions, *An American Childhood* is still a fascinating account of the development of a fascinating mind. It is also an impressive study of the development of consciousness, a favorite subject of Dillard's. Dillard selected her own childhood, she explained, not because she wished to write about her life but because it was the handiest life around. While in many ways *An American Childhood* portrays the youth of an extraordinary person, in other ways the experiences and emotions it describes are universal.

The Recent Years

In a 1987 interview Dillard casually mentioned that she had recently completed the best biography she had ever read—*Henry Thoreau: A Life of the Mind,* by "a new friend," Robert D. Richardson, Jr. (Trueheart, 3). Four months later, in another interview she announced she was divorcing her husband, Gary Clevidence, to marry Robert Richardson in the coming fall, 1988. She explained that a friendship had developed from a "fan letter" she sent him, and after "three lunches and two handshakes" they decided to get married. She continued that although she and Richardson were married at the time, everyone was being "very honorable" about the situation and their divorces were in process (Krauth, 1). Their marriage proceeded as planned in the fall, and they now live together in Middletown, Connecticut.

Shortly before the completion of my manuscript for this book, Dillard's most recent book, *The Writing Life,* was released, in the fall of 1989. It describes the experience of being a writer. "I'm releasing my pent-up wish to overwrite," Dillard promised while writing it. "It's all wildly metaphorical and full of fancy writing" (Krauth, 2). In *The Writing Life* Dillard describes her love-hate relationship with writing and offers details about the process of writing some of her books. Like its predecessor, *An American Childhood,* it delves into the nature of consciousness. *The Writing Life* can also be read as a metaphor for life in general; in this regard it comments on life's ups and downs, the struggle for transcendence, the importance of living fully, the redeeming value of beauty, and so forth. Reviews have been mixed, some critics viewing the book as a sign of Dillard's self-absorption rather than recognizing its more expansive meaning.

Dillard still tries hard to stay out of the limelight. In a 1987 interview she said, "I want enough sanity to keep on writing because it's literature that I love—and that means not being too famous."[17] As a result, she limits her public appearances to two or three readings a year. She still reads voraciously—often as many as 100 books a year, on a wide variety of subjects—and continues to record each one in her journal of "All the Books I've Read since 1966," now in its second volume.

Dillard continues to teach at Wesleyan; her formal title is now writer-in-residence. She hand-selects students for her nonfiction prose seminar based on samples of their writing. The class is limited to 13 students, and some years she turns away as many as 100. She says that when she teaches, she preaches: "It just seems so important to tell them to give their lives to something larger than themselves—to literature or peace or helping others or the life of the senses. . . . The dedicated life is the life worth living. You must give with your whole heart."[18]

On the personal side, Dillard was recently described by one interviewer as "gregarious, funny, careless, wicked and intensely competitive." In the same interview she said of herself, "I often say horrible things that I would like to recall. . . . I don't mean most of what I say when I speak. And the only reason I write, I'm sure, is so I can say what I mean" (Trueheart, 2–3). Dillard's sister Amy has apparently been at the receiving end of some of those "horrible things." When interviewed after the release of *An American Childhood,* Amy remarked of her sister, "She thinks I could put my life to better use." Amy also commented that although motherhood has made Dillard more approachable, she still seems to crave "life in a bubble" (Chambers, 100).

As far as religion is concerned, Dillard calls herself "spiritually promiscuous"; she will attend whatever church happens to be nearby. Although she once toyed with the thought of converting to Roman Catholicism, more recently she has said she is happy with any religion, including Christianity, Judaism, and Islam, but she admits a deep affinity to Hasidism. Despite Dillard's religious liberalism, she has often stated that she has great respect for the fundamentalists and feels they have one up on the agnostics, who have trouble even acknowledging the supernatural.

This, then, is Annie Dillard, both saint and sinner, person and persona, sage and joker. Like a true master of spiritual matters, she always deflects attention from herself. The following statement in a 1978 interview is typical of her humility:

People, holy people, ask me to speak at their monasteries and I write back and say no, keep your vision. In *The Wizard of Oz* there's a giant machine that announces "Dorothy!"; behind the curtain a little man is cranking it and pushing buttons. When the dog pulls back the curtain to expose the little man, the machine says, "Pay no attention to that man behind the curtain! Look at the light show." So I ask the monks to keep their vision of power, holiness, and purity. We all have glimpses of the vision, but the truth is that no man has ever lived the vision. (Yancey, 960)

Chapter Two
We Wake, if at All, to Mystery

Pilgrim at Tinker Creek was not Annie Dillard's first book: her book of poems, *Tickets for a Prayer Wheel,* came out four months earlier in 1974. *Pilgrim at Tinker Creek,* however, is her first major work, and it marks the beginning of her career as a professional writer. It earned her the Pulitzer Prize and focused attention on her life and career. Even more important, it laid the foundation for her subsequent works, providing the crucial framework for her imagery, her philosophy, her theology, and her art.

Dillard has been called "a modern Thoreau" because of the similarities between *Pilgrim at Tinker Creek* and *Walden.* Indeed, her debt to Thoreau is obviously great. Both authors write in the style of a journal that spans a year, both seek to understand God by studying the natural world, and both use a body of water as their central symbol for the transcendent. Because of these similarities and Dillard's frequent allusions to Thoreau and Emerson, critics often make the error of labeling *Pilgrim at Tinker Creek* "good old-fashioned American transcendentalism." A close look, however, reveals a theology less idealistic, more intrinsically mystical, and much less optimistic than transcendentalism.

Theology in *Pilgrim at Tinker Creek*

Pilgrim at Tinker Creek is, as Dillard told her publisher, "a theology book." While it appears to be a book about the natural world, in reality it is about God and his relationship to man. The word *pilgrim* in the title immediately indicates the religious nature of the book, bringing to mind thousands of years of pilgrims journeying to holy shrines. Frequent quotations from and allusions to the Bible, usually the King James Version, also call attention to the book's religious themes. Dillard makes particularly frequent use of the Psalms, Isaiah, Job, Jeremiah, Ezekiel, and the five books of the Pentateuch. The Gospels and Paul's Epistles are also well represented. References to such Christian doctrines as divine grace, Christ's incarnation, atonement through sacrifice, and God's *kenosis,* or self-emptying through the incarnation, also point to the fundamentally theological subject matter of *Pilgrim at Tinker Creek.*

Despite these Christian elements, Dillard's viewpoint is not that of mainstream Christianity. On the contrary, the book presents what must be called a mystical view of life and the creation. Mystics believe in the direct, unmediated experience of the presence of God, called the *unio mystica,* or mystical union. For the narrator in *Pilgrim at Tinker Creek,* nature is often the stimulus that inspires this mystical union, thus prompting critics to label Dillard a pantheist. The philosophy Dillard describes, however, is more accurately labeled pan*en*theism than pantheism. Pantheism views God as immanent in all things, entirely identified with and contained in nature. Panentheism, on the other hand, views the natural world as contained within God but sees God as extending beyond the natural world. Accordingly, the panentheist considers God both immanent and transcendent— both within the natural world and beyond it.[1]

Dillard's panentheism corresponds to Christian process theology, which views God as possessing two very different, apparently conflicting natures. The first is an absolute, changeless, abstract nature, a core essence or state of "being" that remains eternally the same. The attitude of this aspect of God toward man is eternally loving. The second aspect of God is a state of flux, a continual "becoming" that manifests itself as the relative, changing nature of the material world (Richardson and Bowden, 880–85). In *Pilgrim at Tinker Creek* it is this continual flux, the creation and destruction that occurs in the natural world, with which Dillard grapples.

In *Pilgrim at Tinker Creek* Dillard approaches God by using two centuries-old techniques of Christian mystics. In the first seven chapters of the book, as she explained in a 1981 interview, the narrator takes the *via positiva,* or positive way, to the experience of God.[2] Spiritual adepts on this path seek to experience God by contemplating his positive attributes. Dillard uses this technique when she describes the wondrous beauty and intricacy of the creation. She discusses the importance of developing the skill of "seeing" as a means of recognizing and experiencing God in nature. In the sense that *Pilgrim at Tinker Creek* offers guidance for achieving an understanding and knowledge of God, it falls within the genre of the journal of spiritual ascent.

In the last seven chapters of the book, after a mediating chapter, Dillard's narrator travels the more difficult *via negativa,* or negative way, which denies that any conceptualization of God is possible, and which seeks to experience God by completely emptying the mind and the soul. In this view God is so inscrutable that he cannot be grasped by the mind of man. This is the experience of God as wholly "other" than man. In this half of the book Dillard focuses on the horror and apparent mindlessness of the creation and its Creator. In these attempts to explain evil and suffering, *Pilgrim at Tinker Creek* becomes a theodicy. Dillard's greatest theological challenge is to reconcile the apparently opposing aspects of God as the Creator of beauty and the Creator of horror. At the book's end she presents not a simplistic, black-and-white answer but, rather, a remarkable resolution that blends traditional mysticism with modern aesthetics.

Although she labels herself a Christian mystic, Dillard's eclecticism encompasses other non-Christian, esoteric spiritual disciplines. Some of these include medieval alchemy, Jewish cabalism and Hasidism, various Eskimo spiritual traditions, and Islamic Sufism. For example, she calls on Jewish mysticism to help express her concept of the redemption of the material world. According to the cabala, an ancient Jewish system of mystical thought, at the creation of the world some of the sparks of divinity became trapped in the objects of the material world, cut off from the Divine Presence, or *Shekhinah*. The cabalist believed that through prayer the devout person was able to help redeem the world by reuniting his own divine sparks with God, thereby healing the schism between spirit and matter that had occurred at the creation.[3]

Similarly, Dillard refers to the medieval philosophy of alchemy, a complex discipline aimed at spiritual perfection. Christian alchemists of the fifteenth and sixteenth centuries believed that the practice of this discipline, called the Great Work, redeemed the body by uniting it with divine spirit.[4] They called the product of this union the Philosopher's Stone, erroneously believed by the uninitiated to be a magical talisman that turned base metals into gold. Throughout *Pilgrim at Tinker Creek,* references to such esoteric disciplines enhance its spiritual depth.

Dillard's theology is also enriched by the mythical and archetypal nature of the imagery she employs. Sigmund Freud, Carl Jung, Joseph Campbell, Mircea Eliade, and other twentieth-century psychologists and anthropologists have maintained that certain themes recur in dreams, narratives, religions, and myths of both ancient and modern people. While individual and cultural influences create variations in this language of symbolism, the underlying similarities are profound. These themes hold great power over the human psyche because they speak in a language of symbolism that is meaningful to the unconscious mind. Dillard pursues some of these in *Pilgrim at Tinker Creek,* including the quest for wholeness, the rite of initiation into adulthood, and the spiritual transformation.

Imagery of the *Via Positiva*

Dillard begins her pilgrimage with the assumption that God's grace is revealed in the physical world in the manifestation of nature, a basic tenet of Christianity, as well as alchemy. Her central image for God's grace is Tinker Creek, which loops and bends around her. She is grateful that this gift of grace is given freely and without the necessity of merit: "I never merited this grace, that when I face upstream I see the light on the water careening towards me, inevitably, freely, down a graded series of terraces like the balanced winged platforms on an infinite, inexhaustible font."[5] Her response to God's grace, seen in nature's beauty and intricacy, is awe that it is "endless, impartial, and free" (*PTC*, 68). For her the word *grace* elicits connotations of not redemption from sin but merely the limitless bounty given by God, as described in the words of Luke 6:38, "in good measure, pressed down, shaken together, and running over" (*PTC*, 146).

The first aspect of God's grace is nature's beauty. Dillard describes this beauty so strikingly throughout *Pilgrim at Tinker Creek* that reviewers, despite her objections, persist in labeling her narrative style "prose poetry." One of the most frequently quoted of her examples of nature's beauty is her description of the "tree with the lights in it." The narrator reports that she searched for such a tree after reading a description by a young girl, previously blind, who saw a tree for the first time. The narrator finally saw such a tree herself, and it was her own backyard cedar, "charged and transfigured, each cell buzzing with flame." She stood on "the grass with the lights in it, grass that was wholly fire, utterly focused and utterly dreamed" (*PTC*, 33).

Dillard describes the second aspect of God's grace as the intricacy and complexity of nature. *Pilgrim at Tinker Creek* abounds with hundreds of fascinating facts of nature gleaned from the many nature books she has read. For example, a large elm tree, she tells us, may grow as many as 6 million leaves in a season, the ordinary caterpillar has 228 different head muscles, and a single grass plant can produce 14 billion root hairs in four months. The intricacy of nature is also seen in the variety of life-forms and, in some cases, their bizarre behavior. She reports that some species of parasitic wasps etch a mark on the egg of another insect in which they have implanted their parasitic eggs—apparently to warn other parasitic wasps that this egg has already been implanted. After describing a number of unusual creatures and their equally unusual behavior, the narrator expresses her amazement at a creator that will "stop at nothing": "There is no one standing over evolution with a blue pencil to say, 'Now that one, there, is absolutely ridiculous, and I won't have it'" (*PTC*, 135).

Dillard cites the medieval Great Chain of Being and the cabalistic "Splintering of the Vessels" to illustrate the spiritual belief, which she evidently shares, that all the incredible variety of creation springs from a single source in God (*PTC*, 101, 129). She refers to this intricacy as "the world's spotted and speckled detail," an allusion to Genesis 30:32, in which Jacob's pay for tending the flocks of his father-in-law was set at all the "spotted and speckled" animals in the flock. With a little help from God (and genetically controlled breeding), Jacob ended up taking more animals than he left behind. All "the world's spotted and speckled detail" thus represents God's gift of the intricate abundance of the world.

The narrator is positively in awe of the complexity and intricacy of the creation. Dillard adopts an unusual metaphor to illustrate nature's intricacy: the shape of the air around the physical objects of the world. She explains how to create a plaster "sculpture" of the shape of the air surrounding a longleaf pine—pour buckets of plaster into a cylinder built around the tree (*PTC*, 130). Despite the imaginary nature of the resulting sculpture, she makes her point: the objects of creation are complex, intricate, and detailed to the nth degree. She observes that the edges of natural objects, both organic and inorganic, are "fringed," "fluted," "serrated," "notched," and "jagged."

In many cases readers will agree with Dillard's wonder at nature's beauty and intricacy. Sometimes, however, her awe challenges our firmly held opinions about what objects properly deserve our appreciation. Her amazement at and admiration for a copperhead on a rock before her, for example, are emotions many could not share. The feeling she expresses is overwhelming reverence for the sheer existence of life and, even more simply, matter itself:

Here was this blood-filled, alert creature, this nerved rope of matter, really here instead of not here, splayed soft and solid on a rock by the slimmest of chances. It was a thickening of the air spread from a tip, a rush into being, eyeball and blood, through a pin-hole rent. Every other time I had ever seen this rock it had been a flat sandstone rock over the quarry pond; now it hosted and bore this chunk of fullness that parted the air around it like a driven wedge. I looked at it from the other direction. From tail to head it spread like the lines of a crescendo, widening from stillness to a turgid blast; then at the bulging jaws it began contracting again, diminuendo, till at the tip of its snout the lines met back at the infinite point that corners every angle, and that space once more ceased being a snake. (*PTC*, 225–26)

This creative power of nature, for Dillard, demonstrates the unremitting creative power of God. Invoking ancient, feminine symbolism for the creative potential of life, she describes the earth as "an egg, freshened and splitting" (*PTC*, 113). The power of creation "thrusts," "heaves," "seethes," "hurls," and "surges." A tree does not merely grow leaves; it "blasts" into leaf (*PTC*, 99). A million new solar systems an hour are not merely born; they "burst" into being (*PTC*, 97). At the smaller orders of magnitude this creativity is portrayed as a "bubbling" or a "seething," reminiscent of the mystic Meister Eckehart's descriptions of the divine as it bubbles forth from matter (*PTC*, 57, 99, 120).

Dillard illustrates the wonderful generosity of God's grace in nature with a story from her youth. As a child she took pleasure in hiding pennies for strangers to find, drawing an arrow and a message on the sidewalk saying "Surprise ahead" or "Money this way" (*PTC*, 14). These hidden pennies become a metaphor for the hidden gifts of God's grace in the world, which is "fairly studded and strewn with pennies cast broadside from a generous hand" (*PTC*, 15). But while generously strewn, the wonders of nature, like the pennies, are still hidden. They are, she explains, like the line drawings that are puzzles for children: "Can you find hidden in the leaves a duck, a house, a body, a zebra, a boot?" (*PTC*, 17). She agrees with the ancient greek mystic Heracleitus, who, she tells us, said, "Nature is wont to hide herself" (*PTC*, 210).

The difficulties of seeing nature's wonders are many. Some aspects of nature are more than hidden—they are actually invisible. The narrator reminds us that invisible meteorites stream down at us all day long, and she presents the amazing fact that some clouds are invisible except when reflected in water. Nature is a "now-you-see-it, now-you-don't affair" wherein "a fish flashes, then dissolves in the water before my eyes" and deer seem to "ascend bodily into heaven" (*PTC*, 15). There is an element of chance, then, in our glimpses of these wonders. It is necessary to be at the right place at the right time, the narrator tells us. If our timing is wrong, we may miss what we came to see as it disappears "around the next bend." We must be determined and we must be patient. In words reminiscent of C. S. Lewis, the narrator tells us we must "stalk everything . . . the spirit too" (*PTC*, 205). "Catch it if you can," she challenges (*PTC*, 79).

But one who "stalks" God in nature must have still more: the gift of sight. Dillard's recurring imagery of vision is an ancient and universal symbol for spiritual illumination, or divine revelation. This revelation is the real subject of *Pilgrim at Tinker Creek*. Without this gift—another manifestation of God's grace—we are blind, like the eyeless statues she describes that were erected in the Arctic by certain Eskimo tribes (*PTC*, 42). She uses the words of the apostle Paul to state the limits of our spiritual vision: "We see through a glass darkly" (*PTC*, 142). When left to her own resources, she humbly concedes, "I'm as blind as a bat, sensing only from every direction the echo of my own thin cries" (*PTC*, 215).

Dillard maintains that part of our responsibility as human beings is—despite our limitations—to see as much as possible of our surroundings, to "explore the neighborhood." If we can't figure out why we are here, she says, we should at least try to discover "where it is that we have been so startlingly set down" (*PTC*, 12). While many aspects of God and nature are hidden from us, if we carefully cultivate our power of "sight" we will be likely to see more than we might see otherwise. The narrator explains, "I cannot cause the light; the most I can do is try to put myself in the path of its beam" (*PTC*, 33).

Throughout *Pilgrim at Tinker Creek*, Dillard uses light to represent the appearance of God in the world, the moment of revelation for which she waits: "The vision comes and goes, mostly goes, but I live for it, for the moment when the mountains open and a new light roars in spate through the crack, and the mountains slam" (*PTC*, 34). This "inrush of power and light," this "stream of light pouring down" (*PTC*, 7, 2), charges her and infuses her with a spiritual energy that keeps her going long after the vision has ended. She tells us that after seeing the tree with the lights in it the "flood of fire abated, but I'm still spending the power" (*PTC*, 33). This light is the transcendent power of God that momentarily flashes into consciousness and then disappears. The narrator tells the reader in a tone of resignation that it comes just as quickly as it goes, "going on and off like neon signs" (*PTC*, 10).

While the light of revelation comes and goes, the light of divinity's immanence always shines from the very core of matter. This is the light of the incarnation, the continuous presence of God in the material world. To illustrate this presence, Dillard frequently speaks of light shining or glowing within the substance of living things. She describes light shining within the tiny budding leaf of a tulip-tree sapling. The leaf was "translucent, but at the same time it was lambent, minutely, with a kind of pale and insufficient light" (*PTC*, 111). Similarly, a single-celled rotifer under her microscope has a body "like a light bulb in which pale organs hang in loops" (*PTC*, 121). These two recurring terms, *translucence* and *paleness,* become key attributes of matter, connoting the glowing presence of the divine light. Tinker Creek, Dillard's symbol for divine grace, is a primary source of this light, and she describes its water as "saturating cells with lodes of light" (*PTC*, 101).

Dillard also employs the medieval concept of the four elements to show

God's universal immanence. The four elements—air, fire, water, and earth—were believed to be the basic components of all matter in the world. In addition to constituting this basic "physics," the four elements were the foundation for a complex system of correspondences based on the symbolic unity of the number four. The elements were usually shown as part of a hierarchy, moving from the least dense and most spiritual element of air to the most dense and least spiritual element of earth. Dillard's descriptions of the manifestation of divinity in air, fire, water, and earth are an expression of the all-inclusive presence of God in every aspect of the material world, and of a connection between the more ethereal, rarefied spirit and the denser, more substantial matter of the world.

In *Pilgrim at Tinker Creek* Dillard depicts God in the element air as the breath of God and hence the unifying element of all living things. While observing a grasshopper on a windowpane, she is appalled by its machine-like body parts. But when she sees it breathe, "puff, puff," she suddenly becomes, in her own words, "sympathetic" (*PTC,* 64). Air as wind also represents the creative power of God. To illustrate this connection, Dillard reports Pliny's record of the mares of Portuguese, who legendarily raised their tails to the wind to conceive their young (*PTC,* 52). Pliny also believed, she tells us, that plants were impregnated by the western wind Flavonius—an idea that is not so farfetched, since, as Dillard reminds us, the wind actually carries the pollen that impregnates plants (*PTC,* 113).

Ultimately, in *Pilgrim at Tinker Creek* almost everything that lives or moves in the air becomes associated with God. In fact, weather itself becomes for Dillard, as it was for Thoreau, a metaphor for Spirit. She follows Thoreau's lead when she states, "What I propose to keep here is a meteorological journal" (*PTC,* 11). The weather is in her opinion one of only "seven or eight categories of phenomena in the world that are worth talking about" (*PTC,* 49). Since birds travel through the air, they also become representative of the Spirit. Of a mockingbird singing in her chimney, she says that "he strews newness about as casually as a god" (105). She also reminds the reader that in medieval art the goldfinch was often associated with the Christ child (*PTC,* 215). Even starlings partake of the nature of the spiritual. After viewing the passage of a flock of starlings overhead, Dillard seems to be musing on the workings of the Spirit within her when she asks, "Could tiny birds be sifting through me right now . . . ?" (*PTC,* 40).

Fire, the second of the medieval four elements, also possesses a long tradition of association with the spiritual. In the Old Testament it represents the transcendent power of God when he appears before man. God leads the Israelites through the wilderness in the form of a pillar of fire and appears to

Moses as a burning bush. Dillard similarly uses fire, flame, and spark—like light—to portray the appearance of God, but for her they represent the immanence of God in the physical world. To illustrate this immanence, she prefaces *Pilgrim at Tinker Creek* with a quotation from Heracleitus, who portrayed the divine nature as fire: "It ever was, and is, and shall be, / ever-living Fire, in measures being / kindled and in measures going out." The narrator describes this appearance and disappearance of the Spirit as it "rolls along the mountain ridges like a fireball, shooting off a spray of sparks at random." This "hoop of flame" is "the arsonist of the sunny woods" (*PTC*, 76), the flame that lighted the "tree with lights in it" and made the grass under her feet "wholly fire." This presence of divinity within the physical world makes the creation sacred and saves it from the horror of what she calls "the fixed . . . the world without fire" (*PTC*, 67).

The third element, water, symbolizes the gift of life, the very lifeblood of all creatures and the earth itself. The biological necessity of water for living things makes it a powerful symbol for the Spirit. Dillard describes plants and their roots "sucking," "heaving," "spouting," and "hurling" water in the struggle for life (*PTC*, 95, 112, 99). Sharks, the narrator tells us, continually need "new water pushed into their gills." If they stop moving, they die (*PTC*, 98). Since it bestows life, water is another symbol for the abundance of God's grace. Thus, the narrator seeks "live water" and finds it in the form of Tinker Creek, "tumbling live about, over, under, around, between" (*PTC*, 100, 102). The creek becomes the symbol for the incarnation and the immanence of God in the physical world. It is "by definition, Christmas, the incarnation, God's gift to mankind" (*PTC*, 102). The water of the creek also cleanses and purifies. Just as Christ mediates between man and God and offers the forgiveness of sins, so "[t]he creek is the mediator, benevolent, impartial, subsuming my shabbiest evils and dissolving them" (*PTC*, 101).

The water of Tinker Creek floods the narrator's consciousness. She relates that sometimes she is carried away on "that river . . . gasping, lost . . . buoyant, awed" (*PTC*, 82). But this flooding does not drown those caught in its grasp because, as Dillard hints, humankind is inherently spiritual. We come from the water, the world of the Spirit, she seems to suggest. But we have forgotten our origins, leaving the water for dry land and becoming "lost in the leafy interior, intent, remembering nothing." We may visit this land of Spirit/water in our sleep, but in the morning it "heaves" us back on "the sand to the bright light and drying air" (*PTC*, 2). During moments of mystical union the flood of water/Spirit reminds us who we really are.

Like the inhabitants of the air, which become associated with its divinity, the inhabitants of water—fish—take on its spiritual nature as well. Thus,

Dillard's point is once again the grace of God in the form of the bounty of the creation: "To say that holiness is a fish is a statement of the abundance of grace. . . . 'Not as the world gives do I give to you'; these fish are spirit food. And revelation is a study in stalking: Cast the net on the right side of the ship, and ye shall find. . . . They are there, they are certainly there, free, food, and wholly fleeting. You can see them if you want to, catch them if you can" (*PTC*, 186). There is no scarcity of these gifts, Dillard assures her readers. "You'll have fish left over," she promises, in an allusion to the miracle of Christ's feeding of the multitudes with only a handful of fish and bread. By portraying fish, the creation, as "spirit food," she points out nature's ability to nourish us spiritually and to draw us to God.

Another inhabitant of the water, the frog, also appears frequently in *Pilgrim at Tinker Creek*. In Zen the frog represents the essential Buddha-nature, or *Mu*, of all living things. A famous haiku by the seventeenth-century Japanese poet Matsuo Bashō uses the symbol of the frog to illustrate the moment of enlightenment: "The old pond, ah! / A frog jumps in— / Ker-plop!"[6] Dillard parodies this haiku in her description of frogs jumping into an algae-covered pond when the narrator stamps her feet. Her version includes the same sense of joyful humor: "But one big frog, bright green like a poster-paint frog, didn't jump, so I waved my arm and stamped to scare it, and it jumped suddenly, and I jumped, and then everything in the pond jumped, and I laughed and laughed" (*PTC*, 118).

The last of the medieval elements, earth, is the densest of the four. To ancient man the earth embodied the unimaginable creative potential of nature, a force so important it was personified as the first deity worshiped by humankind, the earth goddess. In the Judeo-Christian tradition, as well as many others, earth or dust was the substance from which God created man. Not surprisingly, Dillard uses earth to represent the creative potential of God. In her chapter entitled "The Present" she lists the contents of one square foot of the top inch of forest soil in an attempt to make the reader, and herself, more aware of the thriving intricacy of God's creation. On average, she reports, this amount of soil contains 1,356 living creatures visible to the naked eye, and billions more of microscopic size. "The world is a wild wrestle under the grass," the narrator concludes (*PTC*, 97).

In *Pilgrim at Tinker Creek* another prominent representation of the element earth is the mountain, which, like the sky or air, symbolizes the abode of God. For the Greeks it was Mount Olympus; for the Jews and Christians is was Mount Sinai; for the Muhammadans it was Mount Hira; for the Hindus it was Mount Meru; and so forth. The narrator reminds the reader that "so many mystics of all creeds experience the presence of God on mountaintops" (*PTC*, 89). For herself, we remember, it is from the mountains that revelation comes and "a new light roars in spate through the crack" (*PTC*, 34). Similarly, when revelation ends, either naturally or because of our own self-consciousness, it is the vision of the mountain that we lose: "I drew scales over my eyes between me and the mountain" (*PTC*, 79). Compared with the "active mystery" of the creek's immanence, the mountain, Spirit's transcendence, is "a passive mystery" (*PTC*, 3). The mountain partakes of the essential, unchanging nature of the transcendent, its very "being." Unlike the creek, with its constant change and flow, the mountain "slumbers, blue and mute and rapt . . . it gathers; the world abides" (*PTC*, 201).

Rock, another form of the element earth, is associated with the unchanging nature of Spirit. Dillard portrays rock, or Spirit, as an eternally present foundation always beneath her: "I stand by the creek over rock under trees" (*PTC*, 101). She calls her house by Tinker Creek an "anchor-hold," holding her "at anchor to the rock bottom of the creek itself" (*PTC*, 2). This imagery echoes biblical language referring to God as the rock of strength and the protection on which man should build his life. In *Pilgrim at Tinker Creek,* however, rock and stone are more than metaphors to illustrate the stability of God; they represent the actual presence of God in the physical world. Referring to the Philosopher's Stone that turns all it touches to gold, or divinity, Dillard alludes to the alchemical tradition of the *prima materia,* the formless, elemental essence of divinity that is the ground of all matter.

Dillard's representation of the ubiquitous nature of Spirit reflects the archetypal *Axis Mundi,* or Cosmic Axis, of ancient religion—a sacred pole believed to be the point where God entered the world to communicate with humankind. Ancient people saw many natural and man-made structures as symbols of the Cosmic Axis, such as mountains, trees, pillars, crosses, and ladders. Consistent with this symbolism, Dillard frequently portrays trees as places where God enters the world and enlightens people. It was, we remember, a "tree with lights in it" that gave her one of her first glimpses of the "vision [that] comes and goes" (*PTC*, 33). Likewise, it was to contemplate a sycamore tree, she tells us, that Xerxes halted his army for days, and it was under a tree, the bo, that Buddha received enlightenment (*PTC*, 87). The ancients also used the center of circular or wheel-like structures to symbolize this point of communion with God. Thus, the narrator refers to herself as a spider who keeps returning to the "hub" (*PTC*, 51). The result of all these symbolic references in *Pilgrim at Tinker Creek* is the impression of divinity flowing into the world from an infinity of points.

Despite all these references to God's appearance in the world, the narrator states that she still agrees with Pascal that God is hidden (*PTC*, 144). A

glimpse of God is "the pearl of great price," she tells us: "The literature of illumination reveals this above all: although it comes to those who wait for it,
it is always, even to the most practiced and adept, a gift and a total surprise"
(*PTC*, 33). In an almost-sensual metaphor she describes God as a dancer
"who for my eyes only flings away her seven veils" (*PTC*, 15). God is also
the magician, the hypnotist, and the wizard, all rolled into one: "Some sort
of carnival magician has been here, some fast-talking worker of wonders
who has the act backwards. 'Something in this hand,' he says, 'something in
this hand, something up my sleeve, something behind my back . . .' and
abracadabra, he snaps his fingers, and it's all gone" (*PTC*, 11). This is a
portrait of God as the archetypal trickster, one who appears and disappears
at will, making fools of those left behind and leaving them "dizzy from
head-turning, dazed."

Like many mystics, the narrator admits she has difficulty describing the
experience of the mystical union. She returns from some walks, she con-
fesses, "scarcely knowing my own name. Litanies hum in my ears; my
tongue flaps in my mouth Ailinon, alleluia!" (*PTC*, 33). Clearly, language is
inadequate to describe these moments of communion between human
being and God. Still, the narrator is able to convey a great deal about the
experience. It is, for example, so violent that it leaves the mystic "knocked
breathless," "bashed," "dazed," "reeling," "gasping," and "staggering, as if
you'd been struck broadside by a plank" (*PTC*, 33, 40, 99, 82, 84). It
comes with the force of a tidal wave: "Not only does something come if you
wait, but it pours over you like a waterfall, like a tidal wave. You wait in all
naturalness without expectation or hope, emptied, translucent, and that
which comes rocks and topples you; it will shear, loose, launch, winnow,
grind" (*PTC*, 259).

Despite these terms connoting violence, the *unio mystica* is undeniably a
positive experience. It leaves the mystic "exalted," "exhilarated," "ener-
gized," and "buoyant" (*PTC*, 87, 84, 82). It fills her with joy and makes her
"giddy with praise" (*PTC*, 102). The only appropriate response, she tells us,
is to leap and dance as "King David leaped and danced naked before the ark
of the Lord in a barren desert" (*PTC*, 95). Those blessed by revelation are
unselfconscious in their joy. They become mere instruments through which
the praise of God moves. The narrator described such feelings when she saw
the "tree with the lights in it": "I was still ringing. I had been my whole life a
bell, and never knew it until at that moment I was lifted and struck" (*PTC*,
33). This ecstasy is the *unio mystica*, the goal of the positive path to God. It
is not, however, the end of the narrator's journey; on the contrary, she has
only just begun.

Imagery of the *Via Negativa*

Proponents of the negative way, or apophatic theology, maintain that knowledge of God is impossible, since he transcends the limits of human knowledge and language. They contend that God can be discussed only in terms of what he is not, rather than what he is—thus the label negative theology. Taking this approach, Dillard turns from the beauty and intricacy of nature to its horrors. After examining countless examples of inconceivable suffering, waste, and death in nature, her narrator concludes that God is totally unlike humankind. This realization creates a crisis of faith, for she fears that God is so "wholly other" that he does not care about the fate of human beings, either as a race or as individuals. Dillard commented on this spiritual crisis in her 1981 interview with Karla Hammond: "In the *via negativa* the soul approaches God by denying anything that can be said about God. All propositions about God are untrue. Language deceives; the world deceives. God is not perfectly good, perfectly powerful, perfectly loving; these words apply to beings, and God is not a being. . . . So these people are in an abyss, a dark night. They can only hope that God will find them there— outside the senses, outside reason" (Hammond, 32).

But when God again appears, will he comfort or will he frighten? Throughout *Pilgrim at Tinker Creek,* the narrator acknowledges this frightening side of God. This same Spirit that she "stalks" in the stunning beauty of nature sometimes turns and stalks *her* so that she must flee—in the words of St. Paul and Kierkegaard— "in fear and trembling" (*PTC,* 11). She illustrates this dangerous aspect of God with the Old Testament story of Moses's request to see God face to face. From Exodus 33:20 she quotes God's response: "Thou canst not see my face: for there shall no man see me, and live" (*PTC,* 204). She further describes how God directed Moses to hide in a "clift" of the rock so that when God passed Moses could safely view his "back parts." The narrator admits sometimes feeling the need herself to hide from God "in a curved, hollow place" (*PTC,* 89). She also alludes to this dangerous aspect of God when she speaks of the dangers of looking directly at the sun, "this strange, powerful taboo, that we all walk about carefully averting our faces . . . lest our eyes be blasted forever" (*PTC,* 23).

Dillard also portrays God's dangerous side through the metaphor of the coldness of winter and the northern latitudes. The narrator's desire for a "kind of northing" (*PTC,* 251) is her longing to know God, whatever the cost. The inaccessibility of these northern regions parallels the unapproachability of God, which she compares with the ancient geographers' "ultima

Thule, the modern explorers' Point of Relative Inaccessibility" (*PTC*, 69). Although these northings "draw her," they are full of great danger. "Winter knives," she comments (*PTC*, 42). In the winter almost everything is "dead, killed by the cold" (*PTC*, 46). Dillard portrays the violence of Spirit in the force of thawing ice in northern Canadian rivers—"ripping," "ramming," "punching," "exploding" (*PTC*, 115).

Because Eskimos live in these cold northern regions, they also become associated with God. Dillard portrays them as a more spiritual race, people who live fully in touch with God as nature in both his positive and his negative aspects. The narrator's longing to be an Eskimo is her longing to be more spiritually in touch with God. The Eskimos commune face to face with God, she seems to imply, asking whether "their faces shine too"—like Moses's face shone after talking face to face with God on Mount Sinai (*PTC*, 206). Because of their harsh environment, the Eskimos are comfortable with the negative, brutal side of God as nature.

The manifestation of Spirit as cold in *Pilgrim at Tinker Creek* is not limited to distant northern regions. It appears in the narrator's own valley in the form of "Shadow Creek," the subterranean creek that "chills" Carvin's Creek and Tinker Creek and "cuts like ice" under the mountains. Shadow Creek, a symbol of the dark side of God, is where the narrator sees the horrors that shock her most—the fatal copulation of the male mantis with its murderous mate and the sucking dry of a frog by a giant water bug. Like God's dark side, Shadow Creek is everywhere. Its coldness penetrates every aspect of the narrator's life: "I wring it from rocks; it seeps into my cup. . . . Shadow Creek: on my least walk to the mailbox I may find myself kneedeep in its sucking, frigid pools" (*PTC*, 62).

The hidden and dangerous side of God also appears in *Pilgrim at Tinker Creek* in the form of darkness, shadow, and the color black. We are surrounded by darkness, the narrator complains, but "we're still strangers to [it]" (*PTC*, 20). This aspect of God appears as the death, violence, and suffering that challenge the narrator's view of a benevolent deity. Thus, when she sees a frog collapse before her very eyes, she describes the shape gliding away from the scene as "an oval shadow" (*PTC*, 5). Similarly, the "black," "darkened" body of an unidentifiable water creature disappears in "one ebony fling, a headlong dive to darkness" (*PTC*, 21).

The frog sucked dry by the water bug is one of many graphic examples of the horrors of nature viewed by the narrator as evidence of the Creator's dark side. The food chain, which mankind accepts as totally salutary, is inherently horrifying, as Dillard shows in one example after another. It is a case of "chomp or fast," the narrator quips. (*PTC*, 237). Predation becomes "truly macabre," she comments, when it takes place within families. Musk-rats produce so many litters in one season, for example, that the members of the litter just weaned sometimes eat the newborn (*PTC*, 194). But it is the eating habits of insects that the narrator finds particularly disturbing. The female praying mantis beheads her mate and chews on his neck—while his headless body continues to mate with her for as long as six horrifying hours (*PTC*, 58). But this is no more bizarre than the gall-gnat larvae, which will consume their own mother from the inside out if she fails to deposit her eggs on time (*PTC*, 169).

Dillard finds particular cause for revulsion in parasitism. Ten percent of the world's species are parasitic insects, she asserts, aptly commenting, "What if you were an inventor, and you made ten percent of your inventions in such a way that they could only work by harassing, disfiguring, or totally destroying the other ninety percent?" (*PTC*, 229). She shows the lengths to which parasitism can go in her description of the female stylops. Possessing almost no true body of her own, the stylops spends her entire life as a "form-less lump," absorbing food, her host, through the walls of her abdomen (*PTC*, 232). Dillard singles out the parasitic wasp for special censure, per-haps because of its great number—100,000 species—or its devious ways. These highly successful insects implant the eggs of other insects with some 2,000 of their own larvae, which grow and use the original inhabitants of the egg as a convenient food supply (*PTC*, 167). Such parasitism may ex-tend to the fifth order, parasitic wasps within parasitic wasps within para-sitic wasps, and so forth.

The narrator forces herself to observe these horrors of the natural world because she feels it is her responsibility to learn as much as possible about the "neighborhood" where we've been set down. She concedes that these observations give her "exhausting nightmares" (*PTC*, 12). But her intel-lectual integrity prevents her from turning away, for these horrors present a critical challenge to her belief in a benevolent deity. She must also ob-serve them because her concern is not merely theoretical: at its base is the knowledge that she too is a part of this "universal chomp" (*PTC*, 168). She recalls a childhood experience of watching the egg sac of a praying mantis hatch open in a mason jar. Trapped in the jar, the emerging hatchlings devoured each other, one by one, as the young narrator watched in horror. "We're all in this Mason jar together," she mourns, "snapping at anything that moves" (*PTC*, 239).

Ultimately, it is her own vulnerability to death that unnerves our nar-rator, as Freudians would be quick to recognize. She candidly admits that on the topic of her own death she is "decidedly touchy" (*PTC*, 180). God, as death, is an archer, she laments, "[a]nd we the people are so vulnerable" (*PTC*, 89–90). Death can strike at any moment, and it can come from the most innocent-looking places, such as the pretty wooden birdhouse she once found; it contained, to her surprise, a coiled snake watching her intently (*PTC*, 52). Ignoring the fact of our mortality will not protect us, she declares. Our end is inevitable, for "[t]he world has signed a pact with the devil. . . . The terms are clear: if you want to live, you have to die" (*PTC*, 181). While on the *via positiva*, she watched for a glimpse of beauty that might come from around the next bend. Now, on the *via negativa*, she watches for a glimpse of Death's hem "disappearing around a turn" (*PTC*, 175).

The narrator speaks of death as a defect in the very fabric of creation, a time bomb that could go off at any moment: "That something is everywhere and always amiss is part of the very stuff of creation. It is as though each clay form had baked into it, fired into it, a blue streak of nonbeing, a shaded emptiness like a bubble that not only shades its very structure but that also causes it to list and ultimately explode" (*PTC*, 180). Dillard's portrayal of this "streak of nonbeing" as blue, the symbolic color of the heavens and divinity, implies that God is responsible for its creation. It also suggests that the essence of God himself, as contained within each form, is death. Within this context the "fringes" of creation, which Dillard previously used to refer to nature's intricacy, become evidence of the destructive workings of death through the instrument of time. The narrator laments that "the world is actual and fringed, pierced here and there, and through and through, with the toothed conditions of time and the mysterious, coiled spring of death" (*PTC*, 234).

To illustrate the inescapable horror of death, Dillard uses imagery of human sacrifice. The sea "is a cup of death," the narrator wails, and "the bloodied surface of the earth" is "a stained altar stone" (*PTC*, 174, 219). But the image she creates is not that of humankind in the abstract; rather, the narrator herself is on the altar stone, speaking in language reminiscent of Abraham's near sacrifice of Isaac. She describes herself as "a sacrifice bound with cords to the horns of the world's rock altar," and she is waiting for the worms of death (*PTC*, 242). Death is omnipresent, and human fear of it is never-ending: "We wake in terror, eat in hunger, sleep with a mouthful of blood" (*PTC*, 174).

Interestingly, the narrator never openly considers atheism as an appropriate response to this horror of the human condition. Throughout *Pilgrim at Tinker Creek*, she remains true to her original assumption that a deity exists and that his nature can be discerned in his creation. This assumption forces her to hold God totally responsible for all the world's death, suffering, and waste. If God is present, then his failure to eliminate these negative conditions is blameworthy. If he is absent—Pascal's *Deus Absconditas*—then he is blameworthy for having created and then abandoned the world. From this viewpoint, the narrator's response of anger is wholly appropriate. While she may be playing devil's advocate, her anger appears to burn with the genuine fire of righteous indignation. She turns again to the idea of sacrifice, but this time it is the literal Old Testament ritual of the "heave offering." The reference to her softball throwing arm suggests that she is the offering priestess and that perhaps someday, at her death, her shoulder will itself be the offering:

What I want to know is this: Does the priest heave it *at* the lord? Does he *throw* the shoulder of the ram of consecration—a ram that, before the priest slayed and chunked it, had been perfect and whole. . . . This heave is a violent, desperate way of catching God's eye. It is not inappropriate. . . . God, look at what you've done to this creature, look at the sorrow, the cruelty, the long damned waste! Can it possibly, ludicrously be for *this* that on this unconscious planet with my innocent kind I play softball all spring, to develop my throwing arm? How high, how far, could I heave a little shred of frog shoulder at the Lord? (*PTC,* 264)

This is powerful irony. Dillard transforms a ritual of worship into that common, if childish, expression of anger—throwing something. When the target is God, as here, and the object thrown is a tiny frog shoulder, the gesture is comical in its impotence. But the essence of the narrator's anger *is* her impotence—impotence against all the cruelty, waste, and death inflicted or allowed by God. All of this is potently symbolized by the death of the frog at the "hands" of the giant water bug. The draining of the frog's vital bodily tissues, reduced to a liquid, aptly parallels the draining from the world of God's light-filled presence. What was once utterly full of Spirit now seems devoid of beauty or light. What is left behind, all shadow and darkness, is so alien that it is unrecognizable.

This view is a long way from that of God as a merry trickster who showers beauty and grace on mankind. This God is a "monster" and a "lunatic" who does not care whether we or any other creatures live or die. If there was once a meaning, the narrator ponders, "God absconded with it, ate it, like a wolf who disappears round the edge of the house with the Thanksgiving turkey" (*PTC,* 7). This Creator is so wholly other than man that he sends a shiver down the spine. He is as uncaring as the yellow-spotted dog the narrator encounters one day. The dog is carrying the leg of a deer, whose hoof is "pointed like a dancer's toes." He ignores the narrator as he passes her on the trail (*PTC*, 249). Surely this yellow-spotted dog is the Hellhound himself, the "great dog Death" that does not care whose dance of joy he has ended (*PTC*, 181). This is the "fixed" the narrator rails against, the "mindlessness" she sees at work in nature. This God is so unlike that experienced on the *via positiva* that he indeed seems absent: "The fixed is the world without fire— dead flint, dead tinder, and nowhere a spark" (*PTC*, 67). This horror is the abyss, the void, the experience of nothingness that existentialists describe as angst. In essence, it is the experience of the meaninglessness of life and death.

The language Dillard uses to describe this experience of nothingness is strangely similar to that she uses to describe the experience of the *unio mystica*. Both experiences give her an otherworldly feeling similar to being dizzy, dazed, or dazzled, but the experience of nothingness is clearly more negative. It manifests itself as a fear of falling, which in Freudian terms represents fear of death. The narrator is indeed preoccupied with falling. She imagines feeling her "sweeping fall" as the planet spins on its axis, and wonders what keeps the men at the Palomar Observatory "from falling, voiceless and blinded" (*PTC*, 21, 24). The kayak sickness of the Eskimo took a similar form, "as if he were floating in a bottomless void, sinking, sinking, sinking . . . he just falls and falls" (*PTC*, 22).

Dillard's imagery of physical falling brings to mind the biblical fall of man. It is not the fall into sin she fears, however, but the fall into the horror of life and death. Once again she responds to God by dancing, but this dance is an appalling parody of her dance of joy and praise after the *unio mystica*. She describes this dance as "an eternal danse macabre" that she must perform merely "to keep warm" (*PTC*, 29, 62). "Our every arabesque and grand jeté is a frantic variation on our one free fall," she proclaims (*PTC*, 68). This attitude of despair contrasts so completely with her earlier joy that the reader might wonder how the narrator will manage to escape it. She does indeed escape, but not with any simplistic Perils-of-Pauline deliverance. On the contrary, the narrator must make one more journey, this time on the path that joins the *via positiva* to the *via negativa*.

Imagery of the *Via Creativa*

Throughout *Pilgrim at Tinker Creek,* Dillard hints at a profound unity beneath the appearance of irreconcilable opposites. Her aim is to bridge the seeming chasm between the dualities of good and evil. To join these opposites in a monistic whole, she uses imagery of wholeness, unity, and interpenetrability. Nature's beauty and intricacy on the *via positiva* and nature's horror and death on the *via negativa* are united by means of a third path, which may appropriately be called the *via creativa*.[7] Throughout the book, Dillard's imagery moves toward the unity she sees at the heart of all existence, gradually bringing the reader as well to accept the dialectical tension inherent in this paradox.

Dillard leads to the reconciliation of opposites by suggesting that apparently negative events may in fact have a positive effect. To do this, she shows that shadow, darkness, and horror help to define light, brightness, and beauty. For example, when watching the snow fall one day, she realizes she "could see it only as it fell before dark objects" (*PTC*, 43). Even without resort to the symbolic connection between the cold and God, this observation is an effective metaphor for the power of contrast. In other words, the negative helps to define and delineate the positive. Contrast not only makes the light appear more visible, but it also helps give it meaning.

Dillard also uses imagery of interface and transition—"bridges," "banks," and "edges"—to show that life and death are inseparable. It is on the "edge," or "bank," of an island in Tinker Creek, for instance, that the narrator views the horrifying collapse of the frog victimized by the giant water bug. Dillard labels such violence "real encounters at the edge" (*PTC*, 219), and the place where they occur is to her like a "battlefield" (*PTC*, 4). But it is also at these "muddy edges" of water that "microscopic life abounds" (*PTC*, 119) and under bridges that "an astonishing bloom of life" exists (*PTC*, 19). Death and life "go together up and down the banks," the narrator acknowledges (*PTC*, 266). In her quest to understand God and the mystery of the creation, she is drawn to these "edges" where life and death collide: "I wait on the bridges and I stalk along banks for those moments I cannot predict" (*PTC*, 205). The horror of death occurs in the same place where the beauty of life abounds—the two are inseparable.

Dillard's recurring images of knotting and twisting call further attention to the entwined nature of life and death, beauty and horror, light and dark. There is nothing neat or tidy about the creation: "Wherever there is life, there is twist and mess" (*PTC*, 138). Insects and their parasites, for example, are "horribly entwined" (*PTC*, 230). Parts of the human body are similarly entangled; the Henle's loop in the kidneys, for example, is "rumpled and tangled" (*PTC*, 133). Even the seasons of the year are part of this "mess": after brief periods when "everything overlaps smoothly . . . it all tangles up again" (*PTC*, 75). The handmade cross hanging around the neck of a woman in Peru—"lashed with twistings of vine"—suggests that ultimately our religions themselves are bound up in this same knotting of life and death (*PTC,* 98).

Dillard's images of twisting and knotting finally coalesce into images of circularity, suggesting wholeness, spiritual perfection, and the cycle of birth, death, and rebirth. Thus the narrator's goal is a place where the stars move in "a circular pattern of perfect, concentric circles" (*PTC,* 251). She describes the Spirit itself as "a continuous loop," a "fireball that spins over the ground of continents," and a "hoop of flame" (*PTC,* 76, 90). Virtually everything in *Pilgrim at Tinker Creek*—from the growth of leaves to the movement of earth in space—possesses this same pattern of circularity in its shape or motion. In other words, everything in the cosmos shares in the circular perfection of divinity.

The snakes that frequently appear in *Pilgrim at Tinker Creek* also reflect this symbolism of circular perfection. The mythic *ouroboros,* a snake biting its tail to form a circle, was an ancient symbol of nature's cycle of life, death, and rebirth. The narrator refers to the *ouroboros* when she mentions "the mythical hoop snake" (*PTC,* 76). Dillard also alludes to this cycle in her description of the snakeskin she found knotted, with no apparent beginning or end (*PTC,* 73). The rebirth symbolized by the *ouroboros* occurs when the decomposed matter of once-living organisms is dispersed to become parts of other living or nonliving things. The narrator's dead tomcat has become "the clear sap of a Pittsburgh sycamore" (*PTC,* 98), and the giant water bug, like the frog it sucked dry, is "dissolved, spread, still spreading right now, in the steer's capillaries, in the windblown smatter of clouds overhead, in the Sargasso Sea" (*PTC,* 98).

This regenerative process of nature partakes of the perfection of divinity—despite the horror of death that makes it possible. Dillard alludes to the ancient earth mother goddess to describe nature's powers of regeneration. Believed by religious historians to be the origin of all religion, the earth goddess was often associated with the moon, since its cycles paralleled the journey from life to death to rebirth. The narrator relates the Cherokee story of the moon's cycles: the moon goddess hurls the ball of the full moon across the sky and, after retrieving it, shaves a slice from it and hurls it again (*PTC,* 108). In a moment of mystical ecstasy the narrator unites with this feminine power of the earth in the symbol of grass: "I seemed to be the grass, the receiver of grasshoppers and eels and mantises, grass the windblown and final receiver" (*PTC,* 220). Grass is the "final receiver" because it receives the dead, covers them over with its lush protection, and after decomposition takes them into itself. It is the agent of the process of regeneration.

The narrator finally understands that death is the very tool of the creative power of nature, and therefore cannot be evil. The blood that earlier seemed a symbol of death becomes instead the symbol of life's unity. Even plants share this "blood" in a slightly different form: a molecule of chlorophyll and a molecule of hemoglobin, both appropriately circular, differ only in their central atom, the narrator tells us (*PTC*, 126). The very essence of life unites all living things in an intricate "fabric" of beauty and fullness—a fabric that continues in spite of and by virtue of death. The narrator describes this fabric of unity in a vision of time as a colorful "woman's tweed scarf": "[A]s I looked at the band of time, all the individual people, I understood with special clarity, were living at that very moment with great emotion, in intricate detail, in their individual times and places, and they were dying and being replaced by ever more people, one by one, like stitches in which whole worlds of feeling and energy were wrapped, in never-ending cloth" (*PTC*, 140).

Part of Dillard's purpose in *Pilgrim at Tinker Creek* is to help the reader "see" what she has "seen." She describes her own function as artist in terms of the arrows certain Indians used to track wounded game. They carved long grooves, called lightning marks, down the shafts of their arrows to channel the blood from the wounded animal. If the arrow failed to kill the game, blood channeled along the lightning mark left a trail for the hunters to follow. The narrator proclaims, "I am the arrow shaft, carved along my length by unexpected lights and gashes from the very sky, and this book is the straying trail of blood" (*PTC*, 12).

Thus, it is the work of the artist to point, like an arrow, and to lead the reader to the awareness of God. When the artist achieves her purpose, she strikes her target—God himself—and makes manifest the point where time and eternity intersect. This process "carves" the artist, leaving her wounded and bleeding too, but the wound is a holy one. Like the stigmata, it is the sign of the presence of God. Thus, the "death" or self-sacrifice of the artist parallels death and sacrifice in the physical world: both lead to rebirth and new creation.

In this celebration of the unity of all life and the cyclical process of regeneration, Dillard evidently found a kindred mind in the poet Dylan Thomas. Her chapter "Fecundity" is a meditation on the same themes contained in Thomas's "The Force That through the Green Fuse Drives the Flower." In fact, before its publication in *Pilgrim at Tinker Creek* the chapter appeared in the *Atlantic* under the title "The Force That Drives the Flower." In addition to a shared theme, Thomas's poem and Dillard's book have much common language and imagery. *Pilgrim at Tinker Creek,* however, goes a step further than Thomas's poem. Rather than merely a meditation on unity, it becomes a true journal of spiritual ascent, for Dillard provides the reader with the how-to's of achieving unity, not just a description of her own experiences and perceptions.

Dillard is too humble—as her interviews frequently show—to purport openly to write a book on spiritual instruction; indeed, she expresses dismay at the many letters she receives each year from readers seeking such instruction. Yet despite this humility, she has, consciously or unconsciously, scattered throughout *Pilgrim at Tinker Creek* specific instructions for making the spiritual ascent that culminates in the mystical union. When collected and assembled, these can be presented in a list of 10 instructions that reflect the wisdom of the ancients—what might be called the spiritual precepts of "Dame" Dillard.

First, the spiritual disciple must seek the innocence of a child—"the spirit's unself-conscious state at any moment of pure devotion to any object" (*PTC,* 82). That means being playful, curious, and intently observant. Children, the narrator explains, "keep their eyes open," a prerequisite for finding God in the world. They also pick up anything they see, she reminds the reader (*PTC,* 90). Children have not become jaded; they have not yet committed that gravest of all sins: taking things for granted. The narrator complains that we all start out as infants whose aim is to learn, but within a few years we all seem to have developed "the cocksure air of a squatter who has come to feel he owns the place" (*PTC,* 11). To find God, it is necessary to cultivate in ourselves the child's innocent sense of wonder.

Second, the spiritual aspirant must be courageous and determined. Stalking God is, in the narrator's view, not a sport for sissies: if necessary, we must be willing to lie with our "knees in thorns and [our] cheeks in clay" (*PTC,* 57). We must even be prepared to fight God himself, Dillard tells us. Like Jacob at Peniel, we must be willing to wrestle the angel of God, and to "pursue him wherever [we] dare, risking the shrunken sinew in the hollow of the thigh" (*PTC,* 205). Like the monarch butterfly that climbed hills by sheer willpower, we too must have the willpower to leap whatever hurdles may be thrown in our path (*PTC,* 253). We must be desperate with longing to see God. The narrator describes this desperate longing in a passage reminiscent of the medieval woodcut portraying Ezekiel's vision: "I want to climb up the blank blue dome as a man would storm the inside of a circus tent, wildly, dangling, and with a steel knife claw a rent in the top, peep, and, if I must, fall" (*PTC,* 31).

Third, the spiritual aspirant must live fully in the present. Rather than meditating on spiritual abstractions, we must, the narrator exhorts, become intently aware of the concrete experience of each moment: "Lick a finger: feel the now" (*PTC*, 97). We must become aware of all the living things around us "to try to impress [ourselves] at all times with the fullest possible force of their very reality" (*PTC*, 137). Anything less than total awareness, the narrator maintains, is a waste of time, just "milling around" (*PTC*, 121). The narrator considers such a lack of awareness a lower level of enlightenment, a "dreamless sleep." "Come up a level; surface," she urges her reader (*PTC*, 139, 93). Our intense attention is necessary because this moment, precious in its fullness, is always changing, like a fleeting electron. If we miss the present, she cautions, we miss God's greatest gift, for the present is "by definition, Christmas, the incarnation" (*PTC*, 102).

Fourth, the spiritual aspirant must apprehend the limitations of language and knowledge, elements that cannot encompass God. While language is necessary for creating an awareness of the present moment, the vision of the *unio mystica* is lost, the narrator complains, "the second I visualize this awareness in my brain" (*PTC*, 79). This loss occurs because the nature of language is to divide and distinguish, a process that runs counter to the nature of the *unio mystica*—awareness of undifferentiated wholeness. As the narrator explains, "vision is pure sensation unencumbered by meaning" and "unraveled from reason" (*PTC*, 26, 30). In short, spiritual truth is beyond anthropomorphic notions of knowledge, reason, logic, and meaning. In the narrator's words, "knowledge does not vanquish mystery" (*PTC*, 241). Confronting the limits of language and knowledge forces the spiritual aspirant to abandon analytical thought, which interferes with the vision of unity.

Fifth, the spiritual aspirant must eliminate the consciousness of self that destroys the vision of unity. This exhortation to abandon the divisive influence of the ego is common to all mystical disciplines. The narrator describes this experience as "being emptied and hollow" or as "letting go" (*PTC*, 80, 31). It entails such a "total unself-consciousness" and lack of "self-awareness" (*PTC*, 199, 198) that she describes it in terms of loss: "I had long since lost myself, lost the creek, lost everything, but still amber depth" (*PTC*, 190). Dillard also uses imagery of becoming smaller or lighter to convey the process of emptying the self of the ego. The narrator wishes she could become "lighter" in order to "ride these small winds," like the goldfinch and the feathery down of the thistle seed (*PTC*, 216). This emptying involves a paring down, or a "honing," of the self to its spiritual essence (*PTC*, 33, 251).

Sixth, after emptying the self of the ego, the spiritual devotee must "receive" the world in an attitude of worshipful acceptance. As the narrator states, "I rise when I receive, like grass" (*PTC,* 221). Suggesting the Eucharist, Dillard's imagery of eating and drinking symbolizes this process of taking the world and God into oneself. She quotes Emerson's dream vision of the world as an apple that he was commanded by an angel to eat, just as Peter was commanded in Acts 10:10. The narrator similarly commands us to eat "[a]ll of it intricate, speckled, gnawed, fringed, and free" (*PTC,* 271). We can exclude nothing from this sacred meal, not even those aspects most difficult to accept, such as death. Death is an unwelcome meal—"a sudden stew I never fixed, bubbling, with a deer leg sticking out" (*PTC,* 52). But we must take it in as we take in life, she urges, for the two are part and parcel. Thus, eating the world symbolizes for Dillard, as for Emerson, the total acceptance of God as nature. Ultimately the narrator forgives even the giant water bug. "The giant water bug ate the world" (*PTC,* 271), she finally proclaims, aligning that act of predation with the spiritual attitude that embraces life and death alike.

Seventh, the spiritual aspirant must experience the unity of the microcosm and the macrocosm. Emptying the self into the world and taking the world into the self turns everything inside out. The result is the realization that the microcosm man contains the macrocosm the universe and vice versa. Dillard shows this connection between the outer world and the inner world by pointing out the connection between the environment and the mind of the narrator. When the seasons change, for example, the narrator asks, "Will my life change as well?" (*PTC,* 147) Even further, Dillard implies that perception actually incorporates the object perceived into the body that perceives it. When the narrator views a goldfish, she takes it into herself: "I've an eyeful of fish-scale and star" (*PTC,* 124). Here again Dillard's thought parallels medieval esoteric thought, most notably alchemy. As the alchemy scholar Titus Burckhardt explains, "The highest meaning of alchemy is the knowledge that all is contained in all" (Burckhardt, 75). The ultimate effect of this perceived connection between microcosm and macrocosm is that the outer world appears to be continually pouring into and changing the inner world, and the point of greatest influx is the human mind.

Eighth, the spiritual devotee must master time by taking part in the sacred rhythm of nature's cycles. For the narrator, time's circularity is the key the connection between time and eternity. She describes time as a scroll that is "rolling," "unrolling," or "unraveling" (*PTC,* 32, 140, 256) and as "an ascending spiral . . . like a child's toy Slinky" (*PTC,* 76). This cyclical, rather than linear, view sees each new year as a perfect whole with a new beginning. Similar to ancient people's concept of sacred time, it is the realization that sacred eternity is present in every moment of secular time—the "world without end" of the liturgical "Gloria Patri" alluded to by the narrator (*PTC,* 102, 124). Thus, the narrator takes Marvell's caveat "To His Coy Mistress," "Had we but world enough, and time," and inverts it. With eternity in every moment, there is no shortage of time: "Innocence sees that this is it, and finds it world enough, and time" (*PTC,* 81).

Ninth, the spiritual aspirant must experience sacrifice through death. In all mystical traditions death is the necessary condition for mystical regeneration and rebirth. Dillard integrates the literal with the metaphoric views of sacrifice in *Pilgrim at Tinker Creek* and shows that both physical and spiritual "death" lead to renewal and regeneration. Physical death results in the renewal of the earth through the process of decay. Emotional death, or death of the ego, on the other hand, results in renewal of the spirit. After having gone through her trial by ordeal, after having found herself a sacrifice on the world's altar, the narrator finds herself suddenly free: "the cords loose, I walk on my way" (*PTC,* 242).

The tenth and final step for the spiritual disciple is to become one with the Spirit by sharing in the process of creation. Here Dillard invokes the tradition of Jewish Hasidism to describe the role of the mystic and the artist: the Hasidim believed that through the practice of religion the devout man freed the sparks of divinity trapped in the material world by "uplift[ing] the forms and moments of creation" (*PTC,* 94). Similarly, the work of the mystic as artist is the "uplifting" of the things of creation by pointing out the unfathomable presence of Spirit within them. The essence of God, the narrator tells us, is creativity; God's creation, the earth, floats in space like a work of art, "startlingly painterly and hung" (*PTC,* 268). In the sense that the nature of both man and God is to create, man is made in God's image: "The fact is that we are painters in real life" (*PTC,* 240). It is thus in acts of creation that we live most fully and experience most completely the nature of divine being and becoming. In these same acts of creation we take the mundane, the ordinary, the secular, and, "bearing them aloft," we make them and ourselves holy.

The extraordinary power of *Pilgrim at Tinker Creek* lies in its archetypal roots. The narrator's quest is universal; it begins on the *via positiva* with the search for beauty and unity with the divine. It moves to the experience of death and horror on the *via negativa.* Finally, it culminates on the *via creativa* with God and the individual united in the common joy of creating. The Orpheus myth is particularly helpful to illustrate the role of art in this archetypal quest—a role with which Dillard becomes increasingly preoccupied in her later works. Orpheus, the son of the muse Calliope, was a gifted poet and musician. He succeeded in bringing his wife, Eurydice, back from the dead (although not in every version of the tale) only because he was able to charm the goddess of the underworld, Persephone, with his music. In other words, it is by taking part in the creation through the way of the artist, the *via creativa,* that man is able to transcend death. Through this cycle of death and rebirth, the individual becomes like a god.

In the last pages of the book, the narrator sees twirling through the air a maple tree "key," a seed case, which her mind seizes on as a sign. It becomes for her a lasting symbol of the way of the artist—a symbol that will, in the future, help her find her way back from the *via negativa:* "And now when I sway to a fitful wind, alone and listing, I will think, maple key" (*PTC,* 268). She sees it as "bristling with animate purpose," a reminder of the seed's creative potential. Its spinning movement reflects its circular perfection and wholeness, as well as suggesting the swirling movement of the dervish's spiritual dance of joy. "If I am a maple key falling," the narrator proclaims, "at least I can twirl" (*PTC,* 268). The key is spinning downward but, like the artist, is descending only to rise again, reborn in the tree that will spring from it. Like the seed in the maple key, the artist is pregnant with creative potential and full of joy at the realization of that potential.

In the end, *Pilgrim at Tinker Creek* leaves the narrator and the reader with a radically different view of the world. What lies before her eyes and the reader's is a world that is "utterly new," "ceaselessly bawling with newness" (*PTC,* 108, 145). This newness—and the newness it works in the spirit of one who views it—results from the realization of God's immanence. It is a hierophany that shocks the narrator with the force of its transformative power. "Surely the Lord is in this place; and I knew it not," she proclaims in worshipful awe (*PTC,* 205). The narrator calls this view of the world the alchemist's Philosopher's Stone, the legendary magical stone that turns all it touches into "gold"—that is, divinity. It makes all "transparent," allowing the alchemist to see through the forms of matter to the divinity in all of reality. The narrator describes this vision in imagery reminiscent of the biblical Holy City. The old Lucas cottage is, for the narrator, "my city, my culture, and all the world I need" (*PTC,* 213–14). Far from being a statement of emotional isolation, these words reflect the total connection and perfect unity of the mystical vision. They also reconnect *Pilgrim at Tinker Creek* to Christ's message in the New Testament: the mystical vision is the Kingdom of God on earth.

Pilgrim at Tinker Creek within the American Literary Tradition

Considering the complex themes of *Pilgrim at Tinker Creek,* it is little wonder that critics and reviewers have, from the start, grappled with the equally complex problem of categorizing the book. To describe it, critics often use language that is blatantly hedging. It "blithely straddles the boundaries" and is "not quite" this and "not quite" that, they proclaim in frustration.[8] Focusing on spirituality, for example, members of one school of thought have variously labeled *Pilgrim at Tinker Creek* a religious meditation, a spiritual autobiography, a psalm or hymn of praise, and a poetic-religious essay.[9] Others, concentrating on the nature focus of *Pilgrim at Tinker Creek,* have categorized it as a natural history essay, an environmentalist lyric, and a naturalist autobiography. Still another group, those who prefer to emphasize structure and form, have seen in *Pilgrim at Tinker Creek* a confession, a personal journal, and even a literary autobiography.[10]

Many critics have compared Dillard with such twentieth-century nature writers as Loren Eiseley, Rachel Carson, Edward Abbey, Aldo Leopold, and John Muir. But as her work after *Pilgrim at Tinker Creek* clearly shows, Dillard is not primarily a nature writer. In fact, nature takes a progressively lesser role in her work after *Pilgrim at Tinker Creek.* Even if we look only at this, her first book, we still see many differences between it and the work of those typically considered twentieth-century nature writers. She differs from such writers, for example, in her consistent—even stubborn—devotion to traditional Christianity (although she can hardly herself be classified as a "traditional" Christian). Her concern with aesthetics further separates her work from that customarily associated with nature writing. In a 1981 interview she made the following careful distinction:

There's usually a bit of nature in what I write, but I don't consider myself a nature writer either. Weirdly, I would consider myself a fiction writer who's dealt mostly with non-fiction. The idea of non-fiction as an art form interests me more than anything else. The idea of the non-fictional essay's having the abstract intellectual structures of poetry interests me. Its content is the world. Its content isn't the poet's brain and it isn't the words. Its content is the structure itself and that which is stretched over the structure. The fabric of the surface is the world itself with its data, even, as well as such sensory pleasures as the world's days afford. (Hammond, 35)

Thus, Dillard views nature in *Pilgrim at Tinker Creek* as the means, and art as the end, of her work. It is the presence of such an intention behind and within a work like *Pilgrim at Tinker Creek* that marks the difference between nature writing and literature. Attempting to clarify this distinction, one critic described the literary tradition encompassed by Dillard as "the refraction of natural philosophy through the prismatic consciousness of art."[11]

Dillard's concern with aesthetics is one of many characteristics she shares with the American transcendentalists. Dillard's debt to Thoreau is especially great. In fact, her 1968 master's thesis on Walden Pond points out many characteristics of *Walden* that she would later incorporate into *Pilgrim at Tinker Creek*. Some of these include Thoreau's identification of renewal as nature's primary activity, his concern with the nature of time and eternity, his use of facts of nature as metaphors for spiritual truth, and his constantly shifting perspective as a narrative and tonal device. As further evidence of her debt to Thoreau, Dillard has herself compared her methodology of reading the natural world "as God's book" with the natural theology of the transcendentalists (Hammond, 34).

One of the more insightful discussions of similarities between Dillard and Thoreau is Mary Davidson McConahay's "'Into the Bladelike Arms of God': The Quest for Meaning through Symbolic Language in Thoreau and Annie Dillard." McConahay sees both Thoreau and Dillard as "symbolist writers" whose works are largely explorations in "the explosive potential of symbolic meaning itself."[12] Both Thoreau and Dillard admitted that the nature of language limits its potential to convey meaning, and they both developed the use of symbolism and paradox to greatly expand that potential. In this regard, McConahay asserts, Dillard and Thoreau treat nature and language as similar: they each conceal as well as reveal meaning.

Critics have identified other similarities between *Pilgrim at Tinker Creek* and American transcendentalism, as well as nineteenth-century romanticism in general. Dillard's heightened moments of consciousness, for example, are frequently compared with Wordsworth's "spots of time," and her preoccupation with vision naturally calls to mind Emerson's "transparent eyeball." These and other similarities have caused many critics to go perhaps too far and declare *Pilgrim at Tinker Creek* simply "good old-fashioned American transcendentalism." But the views embodied in *Pilgrim at Tinker Creek* also differ from transcendentalism in several important respects. One difference is Dillard's dialectical approach to the conflict between good and evil. While the attitudes of Thoreau and Emerson toward evil are still being debated, it seems fair to say that both these foremost transcendentalists were more idealistic, more optimistic, and arguably even more utopian than Dillard. Their emphasis was on imposing a positive order on the world through the civilizing power of a properly motivated society. Unlike their optimistic certainty, which acknowledged but rarely confronted the horrors of nature, Dillard's courageous existentialism meets those horrors head-on, finding in nature's impersonal mindlessness an alien essence that confounds all attempts to anthropomorphize it.

In this regard critics often see in Dillard a mind more akin to that of Melville, whose Moby-Dick embodied that same alienness beyond the grasp of the human mind. Both Dillard and Melville challenge the cozy transcendental view of humanity at home in the world. They offer instead a view of human beings as strangers, sojourners, and wayfarers who must forge their own path in a world that is, to use Dillard's term, dazzling in both its horror and its beauty. It is likely that Dillard would also align herself more closely with Melville than with the transcendentalists. In fact, she has often stated that she considers *Moby-Dick* the greatest novel in the English language. In a 1985 essay on her favorite New England writers, she labeled Melville "our greatest artist" but stated confidently that she now found Thoreau "too predictable and too much a kid."[13]

Dillard's work in *Pilgrim at Tinker Creek* must logically reflect the literary, social, and cultural milieu of her own twentieth century, despite the influence of romanticism and transcendentalism on her psyche. The most rational conclusion is thus that *Pilgrim at Tinker Creek* is posttranscendental—that is, arising from but extending beyond that tradition. This is the view of McConahay, who recognizes both the similarities and the differences between Dillard and Thoreau. Playing on Dillard's metaphor in *Pilgrim at Tinker Creek* wherein the narrator describes herself as a ringing bell, McConahay concludes, "Dillard is Thoreau's bell, at once the echo who translates his message and the 'original sound' who forms a new one" (McConahay, 107).

Some of the most interesting commentary on *Pilgrim at Tinker Creek* focuses not on the tradition from which it arises but rather on the tradition it has helped formulate. Viewed from this perspective, Dillard's work fits squarely into the developing contemporary American literary experience. This experience begins with the peculiarly American belief in the ability of the self-reliant individual to make sense of the universe—in short, to determine life's meaning. The quest for meaning often takes the form of the traditional journey into the wilderness—wherever it may be found—where the individual, in solitude, confronts himself and the "other" that is clearly not himself. This encounter with the "other," often in the form of the chaos of nature, forces the individual to redefine himself and the very nature of meaning. He learns finally that his personal identity, like the meaning of life, is the result of a complex process of perception, construction, projection, and ultimately self-creation. This focus on creation, or art—the *via creativa*—becomes both life's how and its why. The artist becomes one of a new breed of inspired priests who create rather than discover truth, not only about the world around them but about themselves as well.

The development of the American literary experience, which parallels the movement of the narrator through *Pilgrim at Tinker Creek,* also parallels Dillard's own literary development. It began with her desire, in *Pilgrim at Tinker Creek,* to find the meaning of the creation. At the book's end she is absorbed in the meaning of the act of creation. This relationship between meaning and creation explains Dillard's interest in fiction, an interest she elaborates on in *Living by Fiction.* Her later interest in the fictions of literary autobiography takes the predictable path to what Albert Stone calls "graphein," or the "strategies of self-composition" (Stone, 2).

An additional influence on these directions in Dillard's career is her role as a woman writer, although by her own admission she is no feminist. In fact, in 1981 she stated, somewhat inflammatorily, "There's no such thing as women's literature. . . . I am an integrationist," and "I want to divorce myself from the notion of the female writer right away and then not elaborate" (Hammond, 35). These comments, as well as her original desire to submit *Pilgrim at Tinker Creek* as though written by a man, have done little to endear her to feminists. Still, her womanhood is and has been an undeniable force in her spiritual and literary development. The spiritual quest has always been a key concern of feminists, stemming from the traditionally female sense of connection and relationship.[14] Dillard's dialectical treatment of good and evil, life and death—what she was perhaps referring to when describing herself as an "integrationist"—is also strongly characteristic of women's literature. Similarly, her emphasis on a rediscovery and even a re-creation of a sense of the self is a particular concern of contemporary women's literature, one that has been especially apparent in the development of the personal diary by women writers.

In the end, little can be gained by pigeonholing *Pilgrim at Tinker Creek* into a single genre or literary tradition, and much can be gained by viewing it from the vantage point of several. Like much great literature, Dillard's magnum opus grows out of traditional forms and structures but transcends them, forcing us finally to label it sui generis.

Narrative Structure in *Pilgrim at Tinker Creek*

As a reader might expect from its many parallels with *Walden, Pilgrim at Tinker Creek* is a highly structured work despite its apparent stream-of-consciousness approach. Just as Thoreau created a cohesive whole from his informally rambling journals, so Dillard has fashioned from her journals an elaborate framework to unify her vision. Like *Walden, Pilgrim at Tinker Creek* is structured around the seasons of the year, in the end returning to its beginning point. We remember the importance of Dillard's recurring imagery of circling, discussed earlier in this chapter. This circular movement in the work's structure similarly illustrates the eternalness of nature's cycles, a quality Dillard associates with the wholeness, regenerative capacity, and perfection of the creation.

Unlike *Walden,* however, which begins and ends in the fullness of summer, *Pilgrim at Tinker Creek* begins and ends in the cold emptiness of January. Dillard's choice of winter as a beginning and ending point serves several important functions. First, it establishes her beginning point as the New Year, a traditional time of new beginnings—an appropriate time for beginning a journey toward spiritual growth. Second, the New Year suggests the entering of the sacred, universal time of ancient man's rituals—Mircea Eliade's *in illo tempore*.[15] Sacred time represents the timeless river of eternity; it is the "place" to which humankind returns to regain connection with the sacred and begin again the yearly cycle that reenacts God's creation of the world. Third, the New Year is shortly after Christmas, the beginning of the liturgical year, the time of Christ's entry into the world. Thus, the narrator's "journey" through the year is a pilgrimage to prepare for the reentry of God into her soul.

Dillard's choice of January as a starting point allows the creation of an additional substructure beneath that of the yearly cycle. Beginning at the winter solstice, passing through the summer solstice, and returning to the winter solstice, the seasons enact a sort of swelling and receding pattern that moves from emptiness to fullness and then to emptiness again. Dillard has stated that this movement parallels the movement of the narrator's soul through the processes of filling and emptying, respectively, of the *via positiva* and the *via negativa*. She describes the book as basically symmetrical, made up of seven beginning chapters about the *via positiva* and seven ending chapters about the *via negativa,* with a mediating central chapter as a transition. The mood and tone change direction in the middle three chapters of the book, moving from a mood of celebration in "Intricacy," to a vague sense of foreboding in "Flooding," and finally to a rapidly intensifying horror and revulsion in "Fecundity." As Dillard describes it, "In 'Fecundity' the downhill journey begins—the rejection of the world. The soul gags on abundance; the mind quarrels with death" (Hammond, 32). By the end of *Pilgrim at Tinker Creek* the rapidly accelerating downward roll has begun to move upward again, and the narrator exits stage left, joyfully dancing to the music of heavenly trumpets.

Dillard's free manipulation of chronology is another important aspect of narrative structure in *Pilgrim at Tinker Creek*. While the book is purportedly about the narrator's experiences during one year of her adulthood, Dillard does not hesitate to incorporate experiences from her childhood or even from other years of her nine-year stay in the Roanoke Valley. This technique allows her to intersperse positive and negative experiences, using the contrast to illustrate the interweaving of good and evil. She sometimes even combines flashback with dramatic foreshadowing, drawing into the present an incident of horror from her childhood: "But this afternoon I threw tiny string lashings and hitches with frozen hands, gingerly, fearing to touch the egg cases even for a minute *because I remembered the Polyphemus moth*" (*PTC*, 59; emphasis added). The effect of this juxtaposition on the reader is the increasing association between the positive and the negative: the apparent innocence of beauty goes hand in hand with horror, and vice versa.

Dillard's use of the first person plays a significant part in the narrative structure of *Pilgrim at Tinker Creek*. While most of the book's incidents probably come from Dillard's actual experiences, it is a mistake to fail to recognize her narrator as at least partially a persona created for specific ends. This mistake has led many critics to complain that the reader does not get to know Dillard as a person or that the absence of other people in the book shows she is antisocial. Such criticism overlooks the fact that the subject of the book is neither Dillard herself nor her fictionalized persona; rather, it is God, as he reveals himself in the natural world. As Dillard has stated, "The first person, as I use it, is merely a narrative device—a kind of floating eyeball, a unifying voice" (Hammond, 32). She sometimes even adopts the implied metaphor of a camera to emphasize the role of the artist-author as objective observer. She "zooms" in for a better view (*PTC*, 57), or has a scene end in a fade-out: "The teacher fades, the classmates fade, I fade" (*PTC*, 60). This dissolution of the narrator's individual personality illustrates the emptying of the self implied by the *via negativa*. This nonjudging, objective observation eliminates the dualistic division of subject and object that arises from the consciousness of self.

In overview, the narrative structure of *Pilgrim at Tinker Creek* parallels the dynamic nature of the creation itself: all things move eternally through the circular, sacred cycles of rising and falling, filling and emptying, living and dying. Dillard portrays this rhythmic motion as the breath of divinity that unites all living things in an eternal circle of creation and destruction. The narrative structure of *Pilgrim at Tinker Creek* embodies this motion in its movement through the seasons, in its movement through the narrator's experiences of the *via positiva* and the *via negativa,* in its movement between the opposites of good and evil, in its movement between the past and the present, and in its movement between the world of the narrator and the world of the reader. Dillard's sometimes-gentle, sometimes-brutal yoking together of apparently disparate things brings to light the subtle threads connecting all existence. She thus becomes the inspired artist, appropriately portraying herself as the spider whose web is the beautiful woven fabric of God's immanence in this time and space.

Technique in *Pilgrim at Tinker Creek*

Dillard's style in *Pilgrim at Tinker Creek* has attracted much critical attention. Its most noticeable characteristic is frequent, sometimes-dramatic shifts in tone, diction, and perspective. A number of critics have condemned these shifts as distracting and inappropriate. Loren Eiseley, for example, took special offense at Dillard's diction in her assertion that "the Creator loves pizzazz" (*PTC,* 146); her use of the word *pizzazz,* Eiseley complained, violates "coherence."[16] Others, however, have praised the "special beauty of surprise" that results from her rapid-fire shifts from the "colloquial and the everyday to the reverential and the celebratory."[17] Thus, the kaleidoscopic impression she creates can be regarded as reinforcing her view of nature and God as disorderly and contradictory.

Dillard's use of contrast helps create a strong sense of irony in *Pilgrim at Tinker Creek.* Although Dillard's narrative persona expresses what appears to be genuine joy at the beauty and intricacy of the creation, she never seems able to forget—nor will she allow her reader to forget—that death and horror are always just around the corner. Dillard uses surprise, understatement, and foreshadowing to maintain this equilibrium between opposites, refusing to simplistically discount one view or the other. The resulting ironic skepticism increases the reader's sense of the narrator's intellectual integrity, thereby increasing the credibility of her theological position.

The prevailing tone in *Pilgrim at Tinker Creek* is familiar and conversational. The narrator frequently uses direct address, as well as rhetorical questions, to speak to the reader. The narrator's easy spontaneity makes her persona appealingly human even though we learn little about her as a person. Dillard's colloquialisms and slang contribute to this personal tone, despite complaints such as Eiseley's about the writer's diction. Sometimes her informal diction creates an offhanded humor, such as the narrator's quip that the purchase of praying mantis egg cases from mail-order houses "beats spraying" (*PTC*, 55). At other times it has the effect of understatement. She comments on the ubiquity of death in the food chain, for example: "It's chancey out there" (*PTC*, 171). She also appropriates words from popular songs. Making light of the horror of insect predation, for example, she comments, "Fish gotta swim and birds gotta fly; insects, it seems, gotta do one horrible thing after another" (*PTC*, 63).

Dillard's sparkling wit adds to the spontaneous tone of *Pilgrim at Tinker Creek*. Her transcendental forebears certainly never envisioned such a lighthearted attitude about life's mysteries—but then they had their idealistic optimism to keep them going. In fact, the narrator's sense of humor often seems the only thing keeping her from lapsing into despair. Sometimes she tells old one-liners that many readers will recognize. But her funniest humor is clearly original. The Law of the Wild, the narrator instructs, is "Carry Kleenex" (*PTC*, 59). Commenting on the unlikely life cycle of the horsehair worm, a cycle requiring a remarkably precise series of occurrences, she concludes, "You'd be thin, too" (*PTC*, 173). The more horrifying the observation, the more likely she is to use humor to help diffuse her uneasiness and the reader's. Describing the gruesome courtship of the praying mantis, she states, "While the male is making up what passes for his mind, the female tips the balance in her favor by eating his head" (*PTC*, 57). Such comments leave the reader uncertain whether to laugh or to cry—Dillard would perhaps approve of both responses.

Yet despite this lighthearted tone, Dillard does not allow her reader to get too comfortable, interspersing her humor and informality with liberal doses of solemnity. Her biblical allusions, paraphrases, and actual quotations are so frequent that a whole volume could be written on her biblical sources. Describing that rare moment when "the mountains part," for instance, the narrator quotes Moses from the Old Testament: "Surely the Lord is in this place; and I knew it not" (*PTC*, 205). Dillard's multitude of other sources—both ancient and modern—also adds to the solemnity of *Pilgrim at Tinker Creek;* she quotes ancient and modern theologians, philosophers, and naturalists by the dozen. The questions she asks are universal in their import, asked by thinking men and women for thousands of years: Who are we? Why are we here? Why is there death and suffering? In addition, the narrator travels the globe for examples of the wonders of nature. Although the action of the narration occurs near the banks of Tinker Creek in the

Roanoke Valley of Virginia, the narrator tells tales of Indian and Eskimo tribes, traces the prehistoric route of migrating butterflies, reminisces about her childhood in Pittsburgh, travels virgin trails with Lewis and Clark, and describes sharks writhing off the coast of Florida. These techniques give *Pilgrim at Tinker Creek* an epic, timeless, and universal flavor, emphasizing the relevance of its message to all people in all times and places.

In addition to Dillard's elaborate use of symbolism to convey her view of God's immanence, she also makes extensive use of other types of figures of speech. Dillard makes especially frequent use of personification, endowing aspects of nature, both animate and inanimate, with human qualities. This technique accomplishes three important ends: (a) it presents nature as full of life's creative potential; (b) by projecting human qualities on nature, it emphasizes the close relationship between man and other aspects of nature; and (c) it presents nature in a more appealing, less intimidating light. Dillard portrays two microscopic monostyla, for example, as little people driving cars: "I keep thinking that if I listen closely I will hear the high whine of tiny engines" (*PTC*, 120). Even the mountains are portrayed in human terms: "The mountains' bones poke through, all shoulder and knob and shin" (*PTC*, 38).

Dillard also makes effective use of strikingly original metaphors and similes, often employing bizarre figures of speech to defamiliarize the familiar. She describes a snake's skin that has been pulled "inside-out like a peeled sock" (*PTC*, 73), water turtles "smooth as beans" (*PTC*, 20), the pages of burned books flaking in her hands "like pieces of pie" (*PTC*, 39), and the ice of glaciers rolling up and down "like a window blind" (*PTC*, 70). The reader's first response of surprise turns quickly into curiosity, challenged to rethink previously automatic perceptions. Dillard goes to great lengths to show the reader new ways to look at old things. She exhorts the reader to "imagine emptiness as a sort of person" (*PTC*, 131) and tells how she renews interest in a given bird: "I imagine neutrinos passing through its feathers and into its heart and lungs, or I reverse its evolution and imagine it as a lizard" (*PTC*, 105). For Dillard such imagery is a mode of perception, not merely an artistic device.

Dillard's frequent use of stylistic techniques associated with rhetoric and poetry has earned her both praise and censure from critics. Several reviewers have recognized a certain extravagance in her prose, a quality they view as an outgrowth of her verdant Virginia surroundings when writing *Pilgrim at Tinker Creek*. Michelle Murray contrasts this style to Thoreau's: "Where the flinty Thoreau is austere, Dillard is exuberant and baroque, as much a part of her lush Virginia valley as Thoreau is of his boney New England soil"

(Murray, 27). Others, however, have viewed this "lushness" as a defect, labeling it "schoolgirlish," "high-sounding murkiness," "adolescent giddiness," and "annoyingly overblown or wispy flights of fancy."[18]

Despite such criticism, Dillard's rhetorical techniques can also be seen as effectively paralleling her themes. She uses rhetorical repetition to illustrate both the unceasing creation and destruction in nature. The tenacity of cicada nymphs, for example, is reinforced by the repetition of the word *suck* (as well as the alliterative repetition of the "k" sound) in the following passage: "They curl, crawl, clutch at roots and suck, suck blinded, suck trees, rain or shine, heat or frost, year after groping year" (*PTC,* 97). Similarly, the destructive force of nature is reinforced by the repetition of *cast* and related ideas in this passage: "There is a sense in which shadows are actually cast, hurled with a power, cast as Ishmael was cast, out, with a flinging force" (*PTC,* 62). Dillard also combines repetition with the use of the present participle to simulate a timeless moment in the eternal present. She painfully describes the unfortunate, deformed Polyphemus moth "still crawling down the driveway, crawling down the driveway hunched, crawling down the driveway on six furred feet, forever" (*PTC,* 61). Similarly, the insistent seeking-after-innocence she advocates is powerfully portrayed in a remarkable series of repetitious participles: "It is possible to pursue innocence as hounds pursue hares: single-mindedly, driven by a kind of love, crashing over creeks, keening and lost in field and forests, circling, vaulting over hedges and hills wide-eyed, giving loud tongue all unawares to the deepest, most incomprehensible longing, a root-flamed in the heart, and that warbling chorus resounding back from the mountains, hurling itself from ridge to ridge over the valley, now faint, now clear, ringing the air through which the hounds tear, open-mouthed, the echoes of their own wails dimly knocking in their lungs" (*PTC,* 82).

Dillard also manipulates word order and syntax to accomplish her ends. For example, she often inverts the natural word order, as when she places an adjective or adjective phrase after the noun it modifies. Thus, she writes, "I don't come to the creek for sky unmediated," and "I couldn't see whether that sere rustle I heard was a distant rattlesnake, slit-eyed" (*PTC,* 89, 20). Sometimes the adjective is placed so far after the noun it modifies that it almost suggests an afterthought, one of perhaps many comments that could be added: "Could tiny birds be sifting through me right now, birds winging through the gaps between my cells, touching nothing, but quickening in my tissues, fleet?" (*PTC,* 40).

Another technique Dillard employs is substituting one part of speech for another. An example is her use of nouns as verbs, as in "Winter knives"

(*PTC,* 42) and "I couldn't unpeach the peaches" (*PTC,* 29). Adjectives, too, become versatile tools in Dillard's hands, and are used variously as adverbs and verbs: red blood cells stream "redly" (*PTC,* 124), and the narrator notices one morning that the grass "had greened" (*PTC,* 108). Other rhetorical techniques appearing in *Pilgrim at Tinker Creek* include ellipsis—"I saw the tree with the lights in it, and my heart [beat] ceased" (*PTC,* 93)—and, occasionally, neologism—as when the narrator imagines the excitement of discovering a new species and having her name inscribed "latinly" in some book (*PTC,* 109). In addition to giving a lyrical quality to her prose, all these techniques help encourage a fresh view of the creation.

So many of Dillard's techniques are associated with poetry that critics often compare *Pilgrim at Tinker Creek* with poetry, some even labeling the work a prose poem. Dillard herself rightly distinguishes her work from prose poetry on the ground that her writing is much more structured than the phrase "prose poem" implies. She admits, however, to an interest in writing the nonfictional essay that has "the intellectual structure of poetry" (Hammond, 34–35). It is therefore not surprising that critics have found similarities between her prose and the work of such poets as Gerard Manley Hopkins, Rimbaud, T. S. Eliot, Henry Vaughan, and Robert Frost.

Dillard's prose reminds readers of poetry partly because of her frequent use of alliteration, consonance, and assonance. Sometimes she repeats initial sounds in a short, simple phrase: "rutted wreck of red clay," "the mantis munching her mate" (*PTC,* 57, 135). Such brief alliteration slows the reader down and draws attention to the alliterated phrase. In other cases the repetition continues longer, lulling the reader into an almost-hypnotic lethargy, as in the narrator's description of bees that kept "fumbling at my forehead with their furred feet" (*PTC,* 148) and in her depiction of moonlight as "the lustre of elf-light, utterly lambent and utterly dreamed" (*PTC,* 70). In still other cases Dillard uses recurring sounds to create an onomatopoeic effect. The recurring sibilants in the following passage, for example, simulate the rushing sounds of Tinker Creek itself: "Long before I could actually see the creek, I heard it shooting the sandstone riffles with a chilled rush and splash . . . as a closed book on a shelf continues to whisper to itself its own inexhaustible tale" (*PTC,* 68). In another onomatopoeic phrase Dillard's repetition of "k" sounds mimics the sound of tree branches striking together in the cold, as the narrator describes twigs that "clack in the cold like tinsnips" (*PTC,* 70).

Dillard also pays much attention to rhythm. In a 1974 interview she admitted, "Rhythm is very important to me. I love to end paragraphs with a feminine ending, and then a long stress for the last word in chapters."[19] She often combines sound and rhythm to create complex poetic effects. For example, the overlapping "g," "b," and "l" sounds in the following phrase combine with rhythm to weigh down the reader like the subject she is describing: "the gluey gobs of bacteria clog the lobes of lungs" (*PTC*, 165). Sometimes the combination of sound and rhythm creates an almost-rhyming effect, as in the following passage: "the coot feels with its foot in the creek, rolling its round red eyes" (*PTC*, 98). Similarly, in the following passage sound and rhythm combine to create a rhymelike effect: "A steer across the road stumbles into the creek to drink; he blinks; he laps; a floating leaf in the current catches against his hock and wrenches away" (*PTC*, 98). The poetic effect is strengthened by the short "a" sound in "laps" that is picked up again in "catches." In another passage, assonance of the short "i" sound emphasizes the near rhyme of "wrinkle" and "dimple," as the narrator describes the leaf of a tulip sapling: "the wrinkle where it folded in half looked less like a crease than a dimple, like the liquid dip a skater's leg makes on the surface film of still water" (*PTC*, 111).

In conclusion, Dillard's style and technique in *Pilgrim at Tinker Creek* demonstrate her concern with aesthetics and the connection between form and substance. Her variety in tone, style, and diction illustrates the kaleidoscopic nature of the creation. Her personification of nature similarly reinforces her view of God's immanence. She uses devices to force the reader to look at the world through new eyes. And her rich lyricism dramatizes her portrayal of nature as itself an artistic creation of the Prime Mover. *Pilgrim at Tinker Creek* is thus Annie Dillard's microcosm, spinning within the vast macrocosm of the world to the unity of its own musical harmony of the spheres—that silent yet deafening sound which unifies and accompanies all the dances of humankind.

Chapter Three
Teach Us to Pray

Annie Dillard's first and only book of poetry, *Tickets for a Prayer Wheel*, might have been overlooked entirely had it not been for the acclaim received by its companion, *Pilgrim at Tinker Creek*. Although *Tickets for a Prayer Wheel* was released four months before *Pilgrim*, reviewers turned to Dillard's poems only after *Pilgrim*'s rave reviews had all eyes focused on this new young writer. It seems certain that the atmosphere of praise—even adulation—surrounding the release of *Pilgrim* created a bias toward *Tickets for a Prayer Wheel*, though just how great a bias is impossible to determine. In any event, several reviewers declared *Tickets for a Prayer Wheel* a virtual masterpiece. It is an "excellent, eloquent book of poems," concluded one. "We have no right to expect this much," gushed another.[1]

Despite this hearty praise, *Tickets for a Prayer Wheel* received only a handful of reviews, compared with dozens for *Pilgrim*. After the initial flurry of attention, critics largely ignored both the volume of poetry and the other poems Dillard occasionally published. One reason for this oversight is the traditionally weak position of poetry in the literary market.[2] Another is that Dillard seemed to consider herself, almost from the start of her career, not a poet but an essayist. In the 15 years following *Tickets for a Prayer Wheel* and *Pilgrim at Tinker Creek* she published six books of nonfiction narrative and many additional essays—but fewer than 20 poems. In fact, in an "Author's Note" at the beginning of her 1982 book of essays, *Teaching a Stone to Talk*, she declared that the essays were her "real work," "not a collection of occasional pieces, such as a writer brings out to supplement his real work."[3] As a result, Dillard's reputation became firmly established not as a poet but as a nonfiction writer, an essayist, one whose work built on *Pilgrim at Tinker Creek*. It came as no surprise when in a 1987 interview she declared that she stopped writing poetry soon after the publication of *Pilgrim*. As she explained it, "My poetry, unfortunately, is no good. I had written poetry and nobody read it, and then I wrote prose and everybody read it."[4]

Dillard overstated the case when she labeled her poetry "no good." And despite the direction her career has taken, *Tickets for a Prayer Wheel* deserves consideration as more than a mere phase in her literary youth. It provides useful insights into the development of her theology and her view of the role of the artist—an issue that becomes increasingly important in her later works. It also helps illustrate her criticism of contemporary poetry, criticism voiced in her 1984 essay "The Purification of Poetry—Right out of the Ballpark."[5] In fact, *Tickets for a Prayer Wheel* exemplifies what Dillard described in that essay as one of the most effective forms contemporary poetry can take, what she calls "the well-made book of poems." A brief look at her essay will provide a helpful context for examining *Tickets for a Prayer Wheel* and her other poems.

Dillard's View of the Role of the Lyric

In her essay "The Purification of Poetry—Right out of the Ballpark" Dillard describes what she views as the two fatal defects of "Modern contemporary" poetry: that it (a) is frequently unintelligible, full of the dense allusions and foreign-language quotations that characterize the work of modernist poets like Eliot and Stevens and (b) usually lacks the substance of those modernist poets, substance that would justify efforts to plow through the apparent unintelligibility to find the meaning hidden beneath. Dillard declares that such unintelligibility in poetry is "an abuse" to readers and "mean." "If you want to enjoy complex and ambitious poetry," she comments, "you might be more tempted to reread the Modernists" ("Poetry," 297–98).

To find the root of these two weaknesses of contemporary poetry, Dillard traces the form's recent history. By the twentieth century, she explains, both epic and narrative poetry had for all practical purposes ceased to exist, leaving one lone poetic genre: the lyric. Dillard points out that traditionally lyric poetry "has been personal, occasional, and meditative all along. . . . [A] certain paucity of intent is simply intrinsic in the form" ("Poetry," 288–89). In the late nineteenth and early twentieth centuries the general trend in all the arts toward emphasis on surface and structure aggravated this superficiality.

The French symbolists also furthered this emphasis on surfaces. Dillard explains that they sought to purify poetry by freeing language from the function of description, making it "evocative rather than referential." The extreme example of this aspect is the poetry of Arthur Rimbaud, whose expressed aim was imagery so vivid that it caused "dislocation of all the senses" ("Poetry," 292). The symbolists exalted the poem as an art object but further detached it from the objects of the world. The resulting deemphasis on poetic content inevitably helped shift the focus to technique.

Dillard does not completely condemn the influence of the symbolists; indeed, she confides in her essay that they "were once all my world." She finds much to praise in the language of French symbolist poetry, including its music, its precision, and its artistic distance, subtlety, and suggestion. The influence of symbolism is in fact apparent in several of her early poems, particularly "Overlooking Glastonbury." In her essay on poetry, however, she concludes that "the Symbolists developed a purified artistic language and did not do much with it themselves." "But the Modernists did a great deal with it," she continues. "In English, Eliot, Pound, Yeats, and Stevens pressed the new polished, broken, and subtle surfaces into the service of metaphysics" ("Poetry," 292).

While Dillard praises the surface technique of the modernists, she clearly does not find in their work the same superficiality she faults in much contemporary modern poetry. On the contrary, she states that "[The modernists'] poetry recreated the breadth and complexity of the great world of ideas and things and added to it the artistic virtue of coherence." Their work, she further maintains, "mediated that relationship which was the Modernists' great theme: the relationship between time and eternity." Nor does she criticize the modernists' use of dense allusions as unintelligible, stating rather that they "educated poetry and pulled it their way, forcing students of the art to learn a new language . . . in order to read their work" ("Poetry," 293). Clearly Dillard finds in modernist poetry the happy medium between the two extremes of superficiality and unintelligibility.

Despite her appreciation of modernist poetry, Dillard saw it as furthering the already-ruinous trend of twentieth-century poetry toward surface and away from content. First, she explains, "a taste for deep metaphysics and a taste for the art of shallow surfaces often go together" ("Poetry," 293). In other words, the modernists sought more subtle forms for communicating their profound ideas. This need naturally created a drive for more effective techniques. Second, the New Criticism, written largely by the modernist poets themselves, stressed surfaces—even more perhaps than their literature—because technique was what they had most to share with one another. Technique was thus the logical subject of the dialogue constituting their criticism.

Dillard explains a third reason the modernists inadvertently helped foster the emphasis on surface that has recently deteriorated into superficiality: the greatness of their poetry far exceeded the talents of those who followed them. Thus, subsequent attempts to reproduce the modernists' complex poetry were largely doomed to failure. The result in many cases, Dillard maintains, was imitation of modernist technique without a comparable body of substance: "One could say that succeeding generations have jettisoned the sweep of Modernism's content and kept the form. One could say that Modernism has become Mannerism and that nothing remains of the art of poetry but language. One could say that today's language is exhausted in surface possibility and weakened in subject matter" ("Poetry," 296).

Dillard quickly backs away from a total condemnation of contemporary poetry, conceding that the mainstream of poetry today is still modernist, and "still absolutely excellent by almost any criteria you choose, past or present" ("Poetry," 296). Nonetheless, she admits to a certain annoyance at a type of poetry often found in the American Midwest and far West that apparently reflects a desire to return poetry to "its putative roots in pantheism" and "subtle emotions." This type of poetry, she complains, often focuses on such insignificant experiences as "the emotion that overtakes one when one notices that the onions have sprouted" ("Poetry," 301). Dillard singles out Gary Snyder as one of these writers.

How, then, does a contemporary modernist poet avoid the Scylla and Charybdis of unintelligibility on the one hand and superficiality on the other? Dillard suggests three long poetic forms that allow the fragile lyric genre to sustain the breadth and depth worthy of the name modernism: the book-length poem, the lyric cycle, and the well-made book of poems. These forms, she maintains, "give all those refined and subtle surfaces something worthwhile to do," and it is by them "that we should gauge the achievement of contemporary poetry, and not by the lorn lone lyric" ("Poetry," 297). It is the last of the three, the well-made book of poems, that Dillard chose for her form in *Tickets for a Prayer Wheel*. Her advice to creative writing students in her classes at Wesleyan provides additional guidance for cautiously steering the middle channel. Poetry is not an outlet for spilling your emotions, she told the reporter Susan Chira in a 1983 interview at Wesleyan. She urges would-be poets to strive for clarity, understatement, precision, and intellectual substance.[6]

Literary Influences on Dillard's Poetry

As might be expected from Dillard's admiration of the modernists, her poetry shows the influence of such twentieth-century greats as Eliot, Pound, and Stevens. This is particularly true of the thematic concerns of her poems. Her title poem, "Tickets for a Prayer Wheel," for instance, suggests the emptiness, alienation, and fragmentation of Eliot's *The Waste Land*. Her narrator, apparently a member of a small Indian or Eskimo tribe that has lost touch with its God, is desperately searching "for someone who knows how to pray." Like Eliot's Fisher King slowly dying from the wound of separation from God, the narrator's family members are dying, one by one, as the narrator desperately struggles to reach God, trying first one type of prayer and then another. The resolution of Dillard's lengthy poem begins when the narrator finally utters the prayer of ultimate humility and helplessness: "Teach us to pray." God's answer comes in the form of a dramatic revelation of his immanent presence in the very midst of the narrator's world. This portrayal of the role of faith in achieving a relationship with God echoes the deep spirituality of Eliot's later works, such as *Four Quartets*.

Other literary influences can be seen at work in Dillard's poetry. Many of her poems, for instance, reflect the musical quality and vernacular rhythms that Pound used so skillfully. She also stresses the effect of differing contexts on the perception and construction of meaning, a concern that frequently was a subject of the poetry of Wallace Stevens. Her approach throughout *Tickets for a Prayer Wheel* and particularly in her poem "An Epistemology of Planets" reflects the interest in viewpoint shown by Wallace Stevens in such poems as his "Thirteen Ways of Looking at a Blackbird." Dillard's intense spirituality and her emphasis on God's immanence invite comparison with a number of other poets. We have already seen the influence of Dylan Thomas in *Pilgrim at Tinker Creek* and, not surprisingly, also find it in Dillard's poems. Similarly, Theodore Roethke's fusion of the physical and the spiritual in the form of woman—a fusion that was the subject of a 1975 essay by Dillard[7]—is a likely source for her image in "Tan from the Sun" of Annie-from-Earth, who "has grit for teeth / and grasses on her chin."[8] Dillard's poetry also reflects the substantial influence of such nineteenth-century poets as Emily Dickinson, Gerard Manley Hopkins, and the French symbolists, already mentioned. The influence of R. H. W. Dillard, her writing instructor at Hollins College and her first husband, has also been mentioned previously.

One final influence on Dillard's poetry is that of contemporary poet and fellow Pittsburgher Paul Zimmer. In *Tickets for a Prayer Wheel* Dillard pays significant tribute to Zimmer in her poem "Tying a Tie and Whistling a Tune, Zimmer Strikes a Nostalgic Note and Invents His Past" (*TPW*, 41). While her poem's title is whimsical, its purpose is far from whimsical and not in the least humorous. It acknowledges the central preoccupation of what Zimmer fans meaningfully refer to as "the Zimmer poems."[9] These poems, which are contained in a number of individual volumes of poetry by Paul Zimmer, nominally have as their subject Paul Zimmer himself. In reality, however, the narrator is merely a persona used to examine the poetic self and the world; the Zimmer of the Zimmer poems is in effect an everyman who, by the very process of remembering his life, creates his own self and his past. The title of Dillard's poem acknowledges this backward-looking "nostalgia" through which all our pasts are invented, and this interest in the construction of memory and identity will appear in some of Dillard's other poems and essays. Other aspects of Dillard's poems that show Zimmer's influence include an identification with nature, a love of trees, an awe and fear of God, an interest in the musical quality of poetry, and a concern with life's cruelty and death.

Structure and Unity in *Tickets for a Prayer Wheel*

As discussed above, in her essay "The Purification of Poetry—Right out of the Ballpark," Dillard maintained that three forms allow the lyric to sustain the breadth and depth of modernism: the book-length poem, the lyric cycle, and the "well-made book of poems." It is the last of these that she has selected for *Tickets for a Prayer Wheel*. Dillard stated in her essay that an analysis of the structure of such a book "reveals the whole as a single broad poem whose parts are named" ("Poetry," 297). On first reading, the 24 poems in *Tickets for a Prayer Wheel* appear more diverse than unified. They encompass a remarkable variety in form, setting, and tone. They vary in length from a mere 6 lines in "Puppy in Deep Snow" to 12 pages in the title poem. Their settings include locations as varied as a forest ("The Dominion of Trees"), the outskirts of the solar system ("An Epistemology of Planets"), a modern business setting ("Day at the Office" and "Eleanor at the Office"), a natural history museum hall ("The Shape of the Air"), and several European and Asian countries ("Overlooking Glastonbury" and "The Boston Poems of H* Ch* M*nh").

The tone of the poems in *Tickets for a Prayer Wheel* also varies greatly. On the one hand, we find the easy colloquialisms of "Tan from the Sun," which opens with a child's joke employing a silly play on words: "Q. Are you tan from the sun? A. No, I'm Annie from earth" (*TPW*, 43). It continues in the same playful tone, contrasting the two almost-mythic characters Tan-from-the-sun and Annie-from-earth. "Words to an Organ Grinder's Music" similarly uses informal diction to evoke the life-style of lighthearted earthiness sought by the drowsy narrator. "All I want's a little comfort," she cajoles her apparent bed partner (*TPW*, 93). On the other hand, some poems in the volume display a great formality of tone. "The Boston Poems of H* Ch* M*nh," for instance, a first-person reminiscence of the Vietnamese leader's youth, mixes impersonal observation with a hint of regret.

"Tickets for a Prayer Wheel" is even more dramatic in tone, voicing the spiritual desperation of the scholar-son of an unnamed tribal society.

Beneath the diversity of these poems, Dillard has forged a unity that justifies the label "a well-made book of poems." In fact, the more a reader studies *Tickets for a Prayer Wheel,* the more its settings, characters, and themes begin to blur. Dillard achieves this effect by repeating specific words, images, and themes to create complex interconnections among the 24 poems. Each poem enriches its companions through a network of associations woven into a cohesive whole. This underlying unity parallels Dillard's overall worldview: beneath the appearance of diversity, all things are united in one spiritual whole. The awareness of this wholeness is a spiritual revelation, a gift of vision that comes and goes, a gift Dillard apparently views as the grace of salvation. This vision is the saving awareness of God's immediate presence that is finally attained by the narrator of the title poem, "Tickets for a Prayer Wheel."

The emphasis on God's immanence is one of many aspects of *Tickets for a Prayer Wheel* that are reminiscent of *Pilgrim at Tinker Creek.* Dillard has herself admitted, "I commonly rob from my poetry for my prose."[10] The resulting déjà vu is pleasant for readers who begin with *Pilgrim* and then turn to *Tickets for a Prayer Wheel.* A good example is the poem "Bivouac," which describes the experience of birth in terms of being heaved from the ocean, the same imagery used in *Pilgrim.* "You wake on the shore," the narrator reminisces, "after waiting for nurse sharks in the sea to heave you toward the light" (*TPW,* 67). Other imagery the reader will remember from *Pilgrim* includes that used to evoke the changing effects of time on the earth ("the ice rolls up, / the ice rolls back"), man's vulnerability to the elements ("You're softshell and peeled"), and the omnipresence of death ("The dead still steer / their sleeping course, / their heels in the air"). The title poem repeats some of *Pilgrim's* most memorable images: the narrator reports finding a deer's leg in the fire, seeing the trees on fire, and being picked up and swung like a bell. Far from appearing repetitive, this "recycled" imagery brings to Dillard's poems some of the same power it created in *Pilgrim.*

The physical structure of *Tickets for a Prayer Wheel* indicates that Dillard intends it to be viewed as a whole, rather than as 24 independent poems. The book both begins and ends with a long, narrative poem in the form of a prayer. These two poems frame the 22 shorter poems that fall between. The first poem, "Feast Days," introduces the main themes of the poems that follow and has as its primary theme the celebration of God's abundant grace. Dillard has divided the subsequent poems into three parts, the trinitarian structure frequently used in the Middle Ages to symbolize the threefold nature of God. The final poem, "Tickets for a Prayer Wheel," presents prayer as the way to approach God and concludes as the book begins, with thanksgiving.

Uniting the 24 poems in *Tickets for a Prayer Wheel* are several major themes. Dillard's thoughtful treatment of these illustrates her intention to avoid the thinness of content of which she complained in her essay on contemporary poetry. The first of the themes she emphasizes is the abundance of God's gifts to man, gifts that take the form of the beauty and intricacy of the physical world. As in *Pilgrim*, Dillard illustrates nature's detail in the image of "The Shape of the Air." She has her readers envision, among other things, the shape of the air inside a bedroom closet, above the entire United States, and around an Indian girl in a birchbark canoe. In "Feast Days" Dillard adopts the newly settled American continent as a symbol of the abundance of nature. Again and again she returns to this vision of the American land as the embodiment of God's gifts. She portrays America as an Eden whose soil is literally bursting with life's potential, the American Indians being God's instruments for bestowing his abundance on the early settlers—in the form of corn, or maize, and the methods for growing it. Throughout *Tickets for a Prayer Wheel*, images of food and eating appear as reminders of this abundance; in fact, "The Man Who Wishes to Feed on Mahogany" is an almost-surrealistic expression of one man's adoration of one aspect of the physical world. Dillard portrays human relationships as still another aspect of the bounty bestowed by God.

A second major theme running through the volume is the pain of loss that inevitably accompanies involvement in life. Dillard illustrates several forms such loss can take. One—the loss of youth, with all its hopes and dreams—appears in Dillard's poems as a cheerless nostalgia that destroys the lust for life. "The Boston Poems of H* Ch* M*nh" is one of the best illustrations of Dillard's portrayal of this attitude. Her substitution of asterisks for the vowels in Ho Chi Minh suggests the omission of the vowels in the Hebrew tetragrammaton YHWH. The subtle implication is that the world leader possessed almost godlike power. But even this great man—who ironically had once been a photo retoucher able to "restore" the youth of his subjects—is now powerless to stop the hands of time. Another loss Dillard portrays is the loss of relationships that do not turn out as planned. In "Arches and Shadows," for example, the woman narrator looks back sadly on a relationship whose outcome is now uncertain. Her embarrassed, almost-sarcastic tone aptly conveys the jaded attitude so often brought by deep disappointment and loss.

Still another loss Dillard describes in *Tickets for a Prayer Wheel* is loss from death. She introduces part 2 of the book with a quotation from the twentieth-century nature mystic John Cowper Powys: "Death-runes, death rumours, ruins and rains of death" (*TPW*, 65). In fact, almost every poem in part 2 deals either directly or indirectly with death. Summarizing this theme is "Farmer's Daughter," in which the narrator speaks of weather as the flux of life, the flood of experience that is beyond human control. It was a flood that killed her father, and now she watches carefully for any change in the weather. Nothing stays the same, she warns: "There's always unseasonable weather" (*TPW*, 85). In "Bivouac" and "The Dominion of Trees" the reader is similarly reminded of life's fragility, and in "Tickets for a Prayer Wheel" the narrator is surrounded by death, confronted with the ultimate extinction of his family/tribe.

A third major theme appearing throughout *Tickets for a Prayer Wheel*, as in *Pilgrim*, is the notion that humankind comes from a spiritual source—one Dillard often portrays symbolically as the sea—but has somehow become "lost" and separated from that source. The result of this separation is an intense longing for reunion with God. Introducing this longing in the title page of part 2, Dillard quotes the Old Testament prophet Amos, who warned that the Lord would send a great hunger and thirst on the people: "[T]hey shall run to and fro to seek the word of the Lord, and shall not find it" (*TPW*, 65). Throughout *Tickets for a Prayer Wheel*, Dillard describes and illustrates this hunger and thirst for God, with strong overtones of the Eucharist.

In "Feast Days" the narrator expresses this need for spiritual sustenance. She voices a deep hunger for God, repeatedly petitioning God to send "food," in the form of Christ the Lamb:

> God send us the springtime lamb
> minted and tied in thyme
> and call us home, and bid us eat
> and praise your name. (*TPW*, 29)

The thirst for God also appears in "Eleanor at the Office." Eleanor is weeping for some unknown reason in a setting that suggests spiritual emptiness and a loss of innocence. Her thirst is so great that she "laps cold water," seemingly insatiable. Similarly, the camel in "My Camel," with its ability to sniff out water in the desert, represents the spiritual part in humankind that seeks God. The narrator describes her attempt to silence this part of herself in the brutal imagery of cutting out the camel's tongue. Despite this violent repression, the camel relentlessly wanders the desert in search of water. Finally, it reaches the heavens, transformed into a source of blessing for the narrator's alter ego, still on the earth below.

Dillard shows the great damage wrought on those who are separated from their spiritual source. In "Feast Days" the apples rotting in the cellar "pray all night in their bins," fearing that in their isolation "they will be neither food nor trees" (*TPW*, 23). A page later, the narrator seeks to return to her own source of spirituality: Tinker Creek. But doing so isn't that easy: the taxi driver she asks to take her to Tinker Creek tells her, "[Y]ou can't get there from here" (*TPW*, 25). Similarly, in "Tickets for a Prayer Wheel" the return to God is not easy. The scholar-son narrator tries one prayer after another to save his starving tribe, desperately seeking to reach the hidden God who is their only salvation.

A fourth major theme in *Tickets for a Prayer Wheel* is the important lesson of immanence, which in effect is the answer to the problems of humankind's longing for God. As in *Pilgrim*, Dillard again asserts that God is in the very midst of our life on earth: "God empties himself / into the earth like a cloud," says the narrator in "Feast Days" (*TPW*, 33). To show that God lives in all things, Dillard portrays inanimate objects as full of life. In "Feast Days" the narrator confides—as though conveying a closely kept secret—that at midnight on Christmas everything rejoices, including soil, freshwater lakes, and sweaters. And in "Day at the Office" Dillard pushes this personification to the point of surrealism, describing, for instance, an envelope drawer as "innocent," curtains as "languorous," and a thermostat as "a child merely, uncomprehending" (*TPW*, 63). Later in the volume, in "Christmas," again the inanimate live. Tin canisters "eat/their cookies," "the curtains moan," and dolls "jerk, breathe and are born" (*TPW*, 102).

This miracle in which the inanimate become animate parallels the miracle in which "life" is brought to humankind through God's incarnation as Christ. In "Tickets for a Prayer Wheel" the narrator, himself in awe, reminds the reader that God, in the form of Christ, really did come to earth and did "eat our food at little tables for a time" (*TPW*, 125). And while Christ the man died and left the earth, the presence of his spirit ever remains. The narrator's family open their money box to find not money but Christ as their treasure. He walks through the house, leaving a trailing "track of flame across the floor" (*TPW*, 125). The presence of God on earth, incredible as it may seem, is for Dillard a concrete, undeniable reality.

The revelation of God's presence, however, is a gift of vision for which we can only wait in patience. Dillard quotes Thoreau on the incomprehensible nature of revelation: "With all your science can you tell me how it is, and whence it is, that light comes into the soul?" (*TPW*, 97). Thoreau and

Dillard thus agree with mystics of all eras that the vision of revelation cannot be invoked at will. Still, Dillard asserts that those who would know God must continue to seek him in every way they can. "Maranatha," prays the scholar-son in "Tickets," quoting the Aramaic words of the apostle Paul—"Our Lord, come!" Desperately searching, he opens door after door and says prayer after prayer. Finally, the last door "flies from the wall" in the explosive, crushing, searing force of the vision of revelation. The narrator's father is granted a glimpse of God:

> God held him close
> and lighted for him
> the distant, dizzying stairs;
> God looped him in a sloping loop of stars. (*TPW*, 123).

Ultimately, Dillard assures us, God holds each individual "close" as he held the narrator's father. His presence surrounds and protects the world and each individual in a cushioning cocoon of love not unlike the encircling presence of air in "The Shape of the Air." The scholar-son in "Tickets" describes this relationship in his sister's dream of a "sculpture / showing the form of God":

> He has no edges,
> and the holes in him spin.
> He alone is real,
> and all things lie in him
> as fossil shells
> curl in solid shell.
> My sister dreamed of God
> who moves around
> the spanding, spattered holes
> of solar systems hollowed in his side. (*TPW*, 127)

This is the view of panentheism, the universe contained in and eternally embraced by God—a God so transcendentally vast that galaxies are but "spattered holes" in his side and so immanently present that "He alone is real." The final words of "Tickets for a Prayer Wheel" describe this experience of being surrounded, immersed, and flooded by the overwhelming nearness of God: "For thou only art holy, / thou only art the Lord . . . / and we are drowned" (*TPW*, 127).

Unity is thus the fundamental theme of *Tickets for a Prayer Wheel*. All things are merely parts of God, as Dillard cleverly illustrates in her poem

"God." She explains that all the numbers from 1 to 10 are pronounced the same, "God," with only slightly different pitches and accents to distinguish them. This is Dillard's way of saying that we are all one—that all we say, do, and are is united within the body of God. Dillard does not, however, discount the individual. "[T]he universal/loves the particular," she tells her readers in "Feast Days" (*TPW*, 33). She maintains, in fact, that the individual is the only way we can view God in our everyday lives. In "Tickets" the narrator's father has learned in his revelation of God that "[God's] hand is his face" (*TPW*, 123). In other words, the way to love God, the universal, is by loving the individual, the particular, in the world. As the narrator explains in "The Man Who Wished to Eat Mohogany," it is love of the things of this world that makes life holy, that makes "Crosses grow as trees and grass everywhere / . . . marking the map, 'Some man loved here'" (*TPW*, 41).

Dillard's Poetry after *Tickets for a Prayer Wheel*

As noted, Dillard has published only a handful of poems since *Tickets for a Prayer Wheel*. One group of these later poems, written in the middle and late seventies, falls into a category of what might be called natural history poems. Each of these poems revolves around a quotation, sometimes quite lengthy, from an old natural history book. Dillard has explained her interest in such old books: "I love their tone, their enthusiasm, their total innocence of moral questions, their pure love of the kind of childish material knowledge that drew so many of us to science when we were young. For me they recapture the innocence of science."[11] Dillard accomplishes some interesting things with these old books, such as using their literal-minded scientific descriptions as sources for sometimes surprising metaphors. In "Light in the Open Air,"[12] for example, careful observation of the nature of light and color becomes a metaphor for the intense awareness of the present moment that she urges. Similarly, in "Monarchs in the Field"[13] literal descriptions of the monarch butterfly create its traditional symbolic identity with the soul.

Another interesting later "poem," in a class all by itself, is "The Sign of Your Father."[14] In a preface to this unusual poem Dillard explains that it is made up entirely of excerpts from the New Testament Apocrypha, which describe a discussion between Jesus and his disciples about the nature of Jesus's teachings. While some might argue that the arrangement of verbatim quotations from another work hardly qualifies as poetry, the effect Dillard achieves is striking. In her "poem" she retains notations—such as ellipses and parentheses—used by the translators to indicate obliterated words or other reasons for uncertainty in translation. The result is a heightening of the sense of mystery already powerfully conveyed by these ancient texts. Particularly tantalizing is a passage about truth, wherein the only words still legible are *do not*, *truth*, and *hidden*.

Some of Dillard's later poems demonstrate the awareness of Spirit in nature so typical of much of her work. These are among Dillard's finest poems, and they present strong evidence to refute her assertion that her poetry is "no good." "Metaphysical Model with Feathers,"[15] a meditation on time and eternity, is particularly moving, with its natural rhythms and sonorous quality. In it Dillard creates the metaphor of time as a wing, "whole and fully fledged." "We live in time's quills as senseless as lice," its narrator proclaims. The poem ends with the same image she used in "Tickets for a Prayer Wheel"—the universe contained in the side of God. The hole in God's side suggests the wound Christ suffered on the cross:

> This is the shape of the one god, holy,
> Who generates the ages, rapt,
> Who tolerates time as a hole in his side,
> A petrel blind and churning. This
> Is the one god, flailed by wings.
> And this is the one time, this raveling hole
> Swift in god and voiceless, black beak shut.

Two more of Dillard's poems that belong in this last category are "Conifers" and "Soft Coral." "Conifers"[16] is a meditation on a quotation describing conifers as "absolute trees." To Dillard, the term *absolute* connotes Spirit, and her focus in the poem is the single-minded skyward growth of the conifer, suggesting both ascent to God and praises raised to heaven. "Soft Coral"[17] toys gently with the idea of a love affair between the narrator and a species of very large coral. Dillard's frequent linking of the sea with the spiritual implies that this love affair represents the fusion of the human being with God in the form of nature. The narrator skulks around the coral for a year before making an advance, reminiscent of the "stalking" of God by the narrator in *Pilgrim at Tinker Creek*. When the two finally touch, the narrator tells us they "rocked the streets of Halifax," suggestive of the explosive force of the mystical union.

Interestingly, in most of her poetry Dillard makes less effective use of poetic techniques than in her prose; in fact, it might even be said that her poetry reads less like poetry than her prose does. To some extent this situation may be the result of a struggle to achieve the natural rhythms and conciseness of modernist poetry. Although Dillard has written some excellent poems, her talent is not well suited to the confines of the genre. As she has herself stated, "[T]here's nothing in the language that poetry can do that prose can't do much better—discursive writing, reasoning, information as symbol, narrative—all those things that poetry has forbidden itself" (Trueheart, 3). This explanation clearly answers the question of why Dillard quit writing poetry. In the end, however, her skirmish with poetry gave her crucial exercise in skills that vastly strengthened her prose. We see throughout Dillard's work, both prose and poetry, a struggle to balance luxuriant exuberance with lucid simplicity. She found the key to achieving this balance in understatement, a technique she employed to stunning effect in her next book, *Holy the Firm*.

Chapter Four
Held Fast by Love in the World

Published in 1977, Dillard's second book of prose, *Holy the Firm*, was not just another *Pilgrim at Tinker Creek*. Readers expecting a second Waldenesque excursion into the beauty and horror of nature were sure to be surprised, although rarely disappointed, by this new work. *Holy the Firm* certainly bears Dillard's mark in many important respects—her naturalistic mysticism, her unflinching intellectual honesty, her concern with the transcendent, and her preoccupation with pain and suffering. It also reflects Dillard's conviction that beneath the appearance of separation a spiritual unity exists that the human mind can sometimes apprehend. But *Holy the Firm* is riveting in a way that *Pilgrim at Tinker Creek* could never be, for it is not about insects, plants, or other nonhuman creatures. It is a true story about a seven-year-old child—the daughter of some acquaintances of Dillard—whose face is burned beyond recognition in a freak airplane accident.

Holy the Firm describes three days of Dillard's life in a one-room cabin on an island in Puget Sound. Part 1 describes the first day, which consists of reflection on the relationship between time and eternity—the problem Dillard had set for herself when she decided to write the book. It also contains musings about the life of the artist and a description of a moth that was caught in Dillard's candle flame one night when she was camping; the burning of the moth powerfully foreshadows the burning of the child, as well as the burning dedication and sacrifice of the artist's life.

Part 2 describes the second day, when the plane flown by the child's father falls from the sky. The child, Julie, is pulled to safety by her father, but a globule of unidentified burning matter flies into her face, horribly burning it. In the remainder of part 2 the narrator founders in a crisis of faith as she struggles, unsuccessfully, to make sense of the accident. She examines and rejects one theological concept after another, finding each inadequate to restore her faith in a loving, caring God.

In part 3 the narrator, reduced to a point of emotional exhaustion by her grief and her intellectual struggle, gives up and gives in to the unknowability of God. This emptying leaves her receptive to what follows: a dramatic personal vision of Christ's baptism on the beach in front of her cabin. This revelation, an experience beyond rational thought, leaves her convinced beyond a doubt of God's participation in the world and of the spiritual unity at the base of all existence. The experience also gives her a personal vision of the role of the artist—a vision that answers the question she posed for herself in part 1. Time and eternity are connected, she concludes, by the life and the work of the artist; the artist is a Christ figure whose dedication and sacrifice bring the spiritual into the material world.

"Nothing is going to happen in this book," the narrator comments early on. "There is only a little violence here and there in the language, at the corner where eternity clips time."[1] Dillard is correct that little happens in *Holy the Firm* as far as traditional plot and narration are concerned. But a great deal does in fact happen, both in the mind of the narrator and certainly in the mind of a discerning reader. The book is tremendously powerful, and, as theologian Frederick Buechner remarks, "the violence is sometimes unbearable."[2] Reviewer Eugene Peterson effectively captures the unsettling nature of *Holy the Firm*, writing that it "wrestles pain to the mat in a wild, unforgettable agon." He suggests that if it were a poem, a good title would be "Annie Agonistes."[3]

Dillard's emphasis on the pain and suffering of a living, breathing human child distinguishes *Holy the Firm* from its predecessor and makes it, as one reviewer observed, "more intensely focused" than *Pilgrim at Tinker Creek*.[4] In the words of the theologian Philip Yancey, *Holy the Firm* also "more directly addresses theological ideas" than its forerunner does.[5] In it Dillard debates such concepts as immanence, emanation, theism, and deism. As a result of this theological complexity, one reviewer described the book as "less penetrable" than *Pilgrim at Tinker Creek*.[6] Dillard is not surprised. Although *Holy the Firm* is her personal favorite of all her books, she has repeatedly insisted, with characteristic hyperbole, that "no one has understood it but one Yale critic."[7] She even admitted in a 1978 interview—with surely some humor and false modesty—that while writing the book she herself had trouble understanding it: "So I'd just keep reading it until it sort of raised my IQ enough that I could understand it and then I'd have to raise it another 30 degrees to where I could generate some more of it."[8] The 15 months it took to compose the 43-page, handwritten manuscript attest to the challenges it presented its author.

Despite Dillard's self-effacing comment that *Holy the Firm* has sold "only eight or nine copies—all to monks,"[9] the book has been widely admired. Reviewers struggling to capture its radiance have described it variously as "a movingly beautiful book," "a diaphanous reverie," "archingly beautiful," and "a rare and precious book."[10] "Transfiguration," the moth essay making up the bulk of part 1, has been reprinted in dozens of writing texts and anthologies. It appears in the 1985 edition of *The Norton Sampler* along with an introduction by Dillard, "How I Wrote the Moth Essay—and Why." In a brief preface Thomas Cooley, the volume's editor, reports that in a recent questionnaire teachers using the book rated Dillard's piece "the most admired essay by a living writer."[11]

Holy the Firm is not what could fairly be called an entertaining book. Reading it is an extremely unsettling experience, but it is also a rewarding one. The following discussion shows why it is my personal favorite.

Emanation, Immanence, and Revelation in *Holy the Firm*

As noted, the central question Dillard poses for herself in *Holy the Firm* is essentially theological: What is the relationship between time and eternity? As she put it in a 1978 interview, "If you examine each day, with the events and objects it contains, as a god, you instantly have to conclude there are pagan gods. And if you believe in a holy God—how does he relate to those pagan gods that fill the world? That is exactly the same question as the relationship between time and eternity" (Yancey, 961). Alluding to Emerson's statement that no one suspects the days to be gods, Dillard appears to be using the phrase "pagan gods" as a concrete image of the profound beauty and power present in the created world of time and space. These pagan gods are to the one "true" God as the secular is to the sacred. They are "tiny" compared with his vastness, but they are by no means insignificant.

In part 1 of *Holy the Firm* the pagan gods—the world of created matter—are more than enough for the narrator. She describes the god of today in majestic terms: "The god lifts from the water. His head fills the bay. He is Puget Sound, the Pacific; his breast rises from pastures; his fingers are firs; islands slide wet from his shoulders" (*HF*, 12). Smaller gods also abound in this world. The narrator's cat drags one into the cabin; he is a tiny but perfect man, with wings that beat in anger against the cat's face. Later he rides naked on the narrator's shoulder. She worships and praises these gods that embody the beauty and majesty of the here and now. Echoing the paean sung in *Pilgrim*, the narrator extols this world of many gods: "Time is enough, more than enough, and matter multiple and given" (*HF*, 29).

In this view of the world, which Dillard equates in part 3 with the neo-Platonic concept of emanation, the world of time and space is irretrievably

separate from God and eternity. The material world has flowed, or ema-
nated, from the one "true" God. But it is no longer directly in touch with
him, "having furled away from him like the end of a long banner falling"
(*HF,* 69). In part 1 the narrator accepts this separation, apparently consoled
by the beauty and intricacy of the natural world. She describes the isolation
of the natural world from the world of Spirit: "I call it simplicity, the way
matter is smooth and alone" (*HF,* 12–13).

Dillard uses the metaphor of physical distance to represent the separation
between the material and the spiritual worlds. The narrator envisions the
spiritual world located at or beyond the distant western horizon, which she
can view from her cabin window. It is literally the "rim," the edge, of the
material world, the "Ultima Thule," the place of continuing creation by or
emanation from God. The narrator sees islands gathering and creating
themselves on the horizon; she is not surprised when she sees a new one
spring into view. She names it "Newborn and Salted," recalling the ritual of
early Armenians and Jews of salting their newborn in blessing and protection (*HF,* 28, 26, 24). This "fringey edge where elements meet and mingle,
where time and eternity spatter each other with foam," is the point where
matter emanates from spirit and where matter and spirit intersect (*HF,* 21).
In ordinary life this point is unreachable by human beings.

Because the world of time and space is separate from God according to
the concept of emanation, the material world is in some respects illusory.
Only the spirit is truly "real." Dillard illustrates this view throughout part
1 by describing the world in surrealistic terms. The language used to describe the god of today exemplifies this dreamlike quality, as does the description of the tiny god carried in by the narrator's cat. Dream and reality
seem to merge, and the narrator sees no difference between them. "Why
should I open my eyes?" she asks while still lying in bed in the morning
(*HF,* 12). The question implies that the worlds of wake and sleep are indistinguishable—both full of dreamlike illusion.

Ideas seem more real to the narrator than objects because ideas are closer
to the world of the Spirit. In fact, during the Middle Ages, she tells the
reader, a man's idea of a thing "was always more real to him than the actual
thing itself" (*HF,* 23). As though to prove this point, later in part 1 she describes walking on a hill as though it were an incredibly realistic perception
of illusion. As she walks, before her very eyes the hill "creates itself, thickening with apparently solid earth and waving plants" (*HF,* 29). She soon finds
herself unable to remember "the real," unable to escape the illusion spreading out in such detail before her. She seems to be telling the reader that each
life is itself a dream vision—Shakespeare's walking shadow strutting his

hour on the stage. The incredible beauty and complexity of the illusion make the human mind forget that it is not real.

Dillard has indicated that part 1 of *Holy the Firm* represents the creation, the emanation from God of the material world (Burnett, 88). Because the world is "far" from the substance of God, of Spirit, and therefore illusory, the creation is also the fall of man into the illusion of the world's reality. The incident just described, when the narrator is walking on the hill and becomes lost in the appearance of reality, is a depiction of the simultaneous occurrence of the creation and the fall. During this incident, Dillard even describes her narrator in terms reminiscent of Adam in the Garden of Eden. She is surrounded by hedgerows, rose hips, thorns, and, significantly, apples. "Already, I know the names of things," she comments, alluding to Genesis 2:19–20, when God brought all the animals before Adam so that he might name them. Already this illusory world seems real to her, so real that she can move and interact with its matter: "I can kick a stone," she rejoices (*HF*, 29).

In part 2, however, something happens that forces the narrator to reconsider this basically emanationist view. It is the tragedy that happens to the seven-year-old child—pseudonymously named Julie Norwich, after the medieval mystic Julian of Norwich. Struck by a flying piece of flaming material when her father's plane "falls" into the world, Julie's face is burned beyond recognition. The emotional horror experienced by the narrator— and, the reader can safely presume, by Dillard herself—challenges her previous, safely held belief that the world of time and space is illusory. It leaves the narrator distraught, sitting at her window, chewing on the bones of her wrist and praying for the comfort of Julie and her parents.

Confronted with the horrifying pain, both emotional and physical, created by Julie's injury, the narrator can no longer believe that the beauty of the natural world, of time, is "more than enough." Nor can she smugly maintain that Julie's life, her pain, and her parents' pain are illusion. The narrator is forced to conclude that even if the experience of life is illusion, love is not illusion. Nor is the pain of loss and grief: "The pain within the millstones' pitiless turning is real, for our love for each other . . . is real" (*HF*, 44). This changed attitude forces a requisite change in her view toward the pagan gods. Whereas she had viewed them as essentially benevolent, rising majestically from the bay or playfully swinging on her hair, she now sees them as the malevolent executioners of pain, the very instrument of time's unremitting assault on living, breathing, feeling beings.

The cruel fate of Julie Norwich thus rekindles in the mind of the narrator her original question: What is the relationship between the one holy God and the many pagan gods? The concept of emanation is no longer adequate for the narrator, because it implies that God has abandoned mankind to the brutal grinding of the "great ridged granite millstone" of time and space (*HF*, 43–44). That abandonment makes God, in the eyes of the narrator, "a brute and a traitor" who has "[slashed] creation loose at its base from any roots in the real" (*HF*, 46). It makes time—in language reminiscent of the runaway carousel of *Pilgrim at Tinker Creek*—"a hurdy-gurdy . . . released from meaning and rolling loose, like one of Atalanta's golden apples" (*HF*, 50). In such a view the one great holy God is isolated and alone, "a holy power burning self-contained for power's sake alone" (*HF*, 48). It leaves mankind at the mercy of the pagan gods of days, who are "without power to save . . . each brute and amok in his hugeness and idiocy" (*HF*, 43).

Although the narrator struggles against the apparent ramifications of emanation, she is equally unable to accept its antithesis, which considers God totally in the world and limited to it. That view, which she equates with pantheism, makes Christ "redundant" and leaves the world "singular . . . and alone" (*HF*, 70). The inadequacy of both these views leaves the narrator embittered. This is her state of mind at the beginning of part 3, as she walks to the store to buy wine for the communion at the tiny country church she has been attending. The irony of purchasing the wine for communion strikes her, and she asks, "Shouldn't I be wearing robes and, especially, a mask? Shouldn't I *make* the communion wine? Are there holy grapes, is there holy ground, is anything here holy?" She cynically answers her own question: "There are no holy grapes, there is no holy ground, nor is there anyone but us" (*HF*, 63).

The revelation the narrator experiences in part 3 makes moot all her prior questions. It is perhaps a response to her decision at the beginning of part 3 to lay aside her intellectual arguments: "I know only enough of God to want to worship him, by any means ready to hand" (*HF*, 55). With this statement the narrator moves into a new level of understanding—one based on faith, revelation, and vision, and appropriately so, for part 3 is the stage of redemption, of doubt resolved and faith renewed.

The vision occurs as the narrator walks home carrying the bottle of communion wine in a knapsack on her back. It apparently occurs on the same hill where she experienced the world's "illusion" in part 1. While that earlier vision was one of separation, she now experiences everything as "whole, and a parcel of everything else" (*HF*, 66). She sees Christ being baptized on the beach before her. After his immersion, "[h]e lifts from the water," just as the god of today earlier lifted from the water of the bay. Each bead of water on his shoulders appears to be the whole world, containing at once past, present, and future. Everything before the narrator's eyes "has fused": "It is the one glare of holiness; it is bare and unspeakable. There is no speech nor language; there is nothing, no one thing, nor motion, nor time. There is only this everything. There is only this, and its bright and multiple noise" (*HF*, 68).

That the narrator's vision is of Christ's baptism is significant, for that event is traditionally viewed as the moment of Christ's dedication to the life of the Spirit. Theologically it is considered the beginning of his ministry and the choice that made meaningful his subsequent death on the cross. That act of dedication transformed his apparently meaningless suffering and death into redeeming sacrifice and salvation. Thus, Christ's passion became a link between time and eternity, a conduit bringing the light of God to the world. The narrator sees the artist's dedication as a parallel of Christ's dedication. This handing over of one's life to a higher power transforms all its sordid experiences into a miraculous bestowing of light on the world. The artist's work drags God into the world: "Hold hands and crack the whip, and yank the Absolute out of there and into the light, God pale and astounded, spraying a spiral of salts and earths, God footloose and flung" (*HF*, 71).

In short, the mechanism of sacrifice fills an action, or even an entire life, with meaning. "Life without sacrifice is an abomination," the narrator insists (*HF*, 72). Throughout *Holy the Firm*, Dillard uses fire as the symbol of this sacrifice and initiation into the life of the Spirit. Suffering gets its meaning, the narrator shows, when it is transformed through sacrifice into the ritual of initiation into the sacred. The fire of the initiation thus lights the world. Similarly, the artist sacrifices his life through his dedication to art. As a result, "[h]is face is flame like a seraph's, lighting the kingdom of God for the people to see; his life goes up in the works" (*HF*, 72).

The narrative structure in *Holy the Firm* parallels the vision of unity Dillard presents. Dillard has stated, for example, that she selected the three-part structure of *Holy the Firm* to represent the Creation, the Fall, and the Redemption (Burnett, 88). The three parts of the book also parallel (a) the three stages of the mystic way—illumination, purgation, and union; (b) the movement of the Christian from faith to doubt to faith renewed; (c) the three days from Christ's death to his resurrection; and (d) the three types of knowing—through the senses, the intellect, and spiritual revelation. All these interpretations embody the traditional Christian symbolism of the number three, associated with spiritual perfection by virtue of the Trinity of the Father, Son, and Holy Spirit. *Holy the Firm*'s tripartite framework is a structural representation of the spiritual perfection Dillard believes under-lies all existence.

Holy the Firm also makes use of the circular movement in time that Dillard employed so effectively in *Pilgrim*. The passage through three days of Dillard's life is a miniature of *Pilgrim*'s progression from winter to sum-mer to winter again. *Holy the Firm* begins on the morning of the first day, moves through the second day, and ends on the morning of the third day. Just as the tripartite structure embodies the perfection of three, the move-ment from morning to morning embodies the perfection of the circle, an-other traditional symbol of spiritual unity. Throughout *Holy the Firm*, as in *Pilgrim*, imagery of circling reinforces this circular structure: burned moths flutter "in tiny arcs," the skies spread "in curves," the light "arches," and so forth (*HF*, 15, 21, 72).

But for Dillard the circle is not merely an abstract symbol of the perfec-tion of a transcendent God. Rather, it represents the very connection be-tween the spiritual and the material, between God and man, between eternity and time. Herein lies the reason for the narrator's search for "Holy the Firm," that hypothetical created substance in touch with the Absolute. If it exists, the narrator asserts, "then the circle is unbroken" (*HF*, 70). By the book's end, the narrator has found and identified "Holy the Firm"—it is the artist himself and his work: "He is holy and he is firm, spanning all the long gap with the length of his love, in flawed imitation of Christ on the cross stretched both ways unbroken and thorned. So must the work be also, in touch with, in touch with, in touch with; spanning the gap, from here to eternity, home" (*HF*, 72).

The identification of the artist as the Christ figure who links heaven and earth sheds additional light on Dillard's selection of morning as the begin-ning and ending point of *Holy the Firm*. Morning is the time of the rising of the sun, which in Christian tradition has long been associated with Christ's resurrection, the coming of spiritual light, and a time of new beginnings. Christ is himself referred to in the New Testament as the "Day Star" (2 Pet. 1:19) and the "Morning Star" (Rev. 22:16). The rising sun is also associated with baptism: members of some Christian denominations, both in ancient and in modern times, face the east during the ritual of baptism. Not sur-prisingly, then, it is in the morning that Dillard experiences her own dra-matic vision as she meets Christ in the morning sun and in her own rising art. Later in the part 3 she promises the absent child Julie this same joy of being touched, even burned, by God's presence in the morning: "[M]ornings, you won't be able to walk for the power of it" (*HF*, 75). The presence and power of God are most palpable in the morning, she seems to intimate.

Dillard has constructed *Holy the Firm* with the care of a serious artist, taking great pains to express as much with her structure as with her words themselves. It is this care that takes her work beyond that of a theologian or a philosopher. *Holy the Firm* is Dillard's statement that her aesthetic purpose as an artist is also a spiritual mission. Throughout the book, she uses striking metaphors to drive home this vision of the artist as savior of the world. These metaphors portray the artist as a burning moth caught in a candle, as the burned child Julie Norwich, as a nun married to Christ, as a prophet or visionary, as Mary the mother of Christ, and finally as Christ himself. The following section touches briefly on Dillard's treatment of each of these images.

Images of the Artist in *Holy the Firm*

Dillard has admitted that *Holy the Firm* is "freighted with heavy-handed symbolism"; almost all of that symbolism consists of imagery describing the role of the artist. In her essay "How I Wrote the Moth Essay—and Why" she explains that *Holy the Firm* arose from her life situation after the publication of *Pilgrim at Tinker Creek*. She explains that she was in a very real sense attempting to escape the fame that had invaded her life after winning the Pulitzer Prize. She was essentially alone, having recently divorced her husband and moved to the Puget Sound area to teach poetry at Western Washington University. She concludes, "These, then, were issues for me at that time: dedication, purity, sacrifice" ("How I Wrote," 20, 14).

Like many of the incidents described in Dillard's works, the burning of the moth described in part 1 of *Holy the Firm* was an actual occurrence. As Dillard explains in *Holy the Firm*, it had happened two years earlier when she still lived in Virginia, while on a camping trip by herself. In an attempt to renew her dedication to her art, she was rereading James Ramsey Ullman's *The Day on Fire*, about the life of Rimbaud. While she read in the evening by candlelight, moths kept flying into her candle. Many managed to escape only slightly singed, but one particularly large golden moth—which Dillard identified as female—was caught in the flame. After her body was engulfed in flame, she became in effect a second wick, burning and shedding her own light for two hours, until Dillard blew her out. The experience so struck Dillard that she wrote about it in her ever-present journal, to which she turned two years later when she decided to write the moth essay.

In *Holy the Firm* Dillard devotes two full pages to the description of the burning of the moth. The central image of the book, this description contains much of the striking prose so praised by the book's reviewers. For sheer visual force it rivals Dillard's descriptions in *Pilgrim at Tinker Creek* of the collapsing frog and the tree with the lights in it. Here is an excerpt:

She kept burning. The wax rose in the moth's body from her soaking abdomen to her thorax to the jagged hole where her head should be, and widened into flame, a saffron-yellow flame that robed her to the ground like any immolating monk. That candle had two wicks, two flames of identical height, side by side. The moth's head was fire. She burned for two hours, until I blew her out. She burned for two hours without changing, without bending or leaning—only glowing within, like a building fire glimpsed through silhouetted walls, like a hollow saint, like a flame-faced virgin gone to God, while I read by her light, kindled, while Rimbaud in Paris burnt out his brains in a thousand poems, while night pooled wetly at my feet. (*HF*, 17)

The burning moth is for many reasons a particularly rich metaphor, and it creates in *Holy the Firm* a wealth of associations. Like the butterfly, the moth is an ancient symbol for the human soul. Its ability to fly and its attraction to light make it an especially appropriate symbol of the soul that is drawn to God. More specifically, the moth that flies into the narrator's candle flame is golden, and it is female. Dillard makes it especially clear that both she and the child Julie Norwich are blond, as is the narrator's yellow cat, Small.[12] Throughout *Holy the Firm*, Dillard draws connections between these four—herself, the child, the cat, and the moth—for the primary purpose of illustrating her view of the role of the artist.

These "characters" all share with the moth the fact of their burning, either literally or figuratively. The yellow cat Small once burned her tail in one of the narrator's candles; Julie had her face burned off in the plane accident; and the narrator burns for God and for her art. Their yellow hair—or fur—can even be viewed figuratively as a reference to that burning. Fire is an important image in *Holy the Firm*, as it was in *Pilgrim*. But there it was almost exclusively a positive image, while here it is strangely contradictory. In a negative sense, fire connotes physical pain, suffering, and even death. This meaning is evident in the case of the child Julie, whose physical pain Dillard describes in brutal, even gruesome terms. Pain medication does not work for severe burn victims, she relates, because without skin the drugs simply seep out of the body and dissolve into the sheets. "Can you scream without lips?" she queries, graphically driving home the suffering of this innocent victim of a tragic accident (*HF,* 36). Burning also suggests the ancient ritual of sacrifice, which entails the giving of one life to bring supposed good to others. Dillard bitterly suggests that the child has been sacrificed by God to remind mankind of his power and might.

In contrast to the child's physical burning, the artist's burning is figurative. It consists of emotional pain, most notably the pain of loneliness. The artist in many ways is isolated because of what might be called her mission in life. The narrator is physically alone, without a husband or mate, and while she does not specifically state the reason for her solitary life, she allows her reader to believe it is because the artist must be alone. While she accepts her solitariness as a necessary part of the artist's life, it seems to cause her pain; she associates aloneness with sterility and the failure to procreate. The narrator expresses concern, for instance, about whether the burned moth had laid its eggs before its death in the flame and about whether Julie, now horribly scarred, will ever find a husband to love her. Another of the narrator's alter egos, the yellow cat Small, has completely lost her ability to reproduce, having only recently been neutered. She chews at her stitches, as though in complaint about her new limitation.

In addition to being deprived of a normal family life, the artist must suffer isolation from other human beings who are unable to understand her vision and her drive to share it. This drive is all-consuming and takes every ounce of the artist's energy. The narrator rails at the innocence of the students in her poetry class who believe they can be writers without sacrifice: "I tried to tell them what the choice meant: you can't be anything else. You must go at your life with a broadax" (*HF,* 18). Dillard's meaning is clear: the artist must sacrifice everything, as the narrator has. Sacrifice is not an incidental result of the artist's mission; it is an intrinsic part of that mission. It comes with the territory.

This emotional pain of the artist is no less severe, Dillard implies, than the physical pain of the burned child—and in some ways it is worse than the child's pain. Julie's wounds will someday heal, and her pain will cease; someday she will even have a husband and her own children. The narrator addresses the absent child: "This will all be a dream, an anecdote, something to tell your husband one night" (*HF,* 76). The pain of the artist, on the other hand, will never end; it will burn as long as she lives. In place of a family and natural human intercourse, she will have the society only of Small, the pet she disparagingly refers to as "this wretched cat" (*HF,* 45). She will probably even outlive the cat, she grumbles, and have to replace her with another. As if to drive home this point, Dillard describes Julie trying to play with Small, treating her like a doll and dressing her in doll clothes. The cat resists her efforts and tries to run away, refusing to play "child" for the frustrated Julie. The cat is no better "child" for the narrator; it is a poor substitute for a flesh-and-blood child, for the joy of family life, and for normal human interaction.

Fire and burning also have a positive connotation in *Holy the Firm*. In this sense fire connotes illumination, enlightenment, purification, and even initiation. The pain of the artist, her very burning, is the stuff from which her creativity flows, illuminating the world with the light of her burning. The narrator exclaims, "What can any artist set on fire but his own world?" (*HF*, 72). This burning of the artist, then, is not meaningless suffering but the result of a conscious choice to dedicate her life to art—the connecting point between time and eternity, between man and God. This dedication transforms her suffering into a sacrifice with profound spiritual import. No mere victim, the narrator has become by this act the agent of God's glory, entrusted with the mission of bringing spiritual light into the world.

In this sense fire in *Holy the Firm* is thus a symbol of the initiation of the artist into the spiritual life. It represents a burning away of the old life and a baptism into the new life. It is the Pentecostal fire, the "baptism by fire" of which Christ spoke in the New Testament. It begins with suffering and death of the self and ends in total rebirth. Indeed, the original cover of *Holy the Firm* bears a drawing of a flaming phoenix, the legendary bird that every 500 years burned itself to death and then arose, reborn, from its own ashes. *Holy the Firm* is in some ways the record of Dillard's own burning to ashes and, finally, her rebirth from them into a new life.

Dillard uses additional imagery to illustrate this rebirth into a new spiritual life. As noted, she frequently mentions salt, alluding to the ancient practice of salting the newborn and to the modern Roman Catholic practice of placing salt in the mouth of an infant being baptized (*HF*, 24–25). She combines the fire and salt imagery in a powerful description of the initiation of the child Julie into the spiritual life: "Julie Norwich is salted with fire. She is preserved like a salted fillet from all evil, baptized at birth into time and now into eternity, into the bladelike arms of God" (*HF*, 74).

The imagery of initiation is related to imagery implying loss or death of the self. After describing Julie's face as "slaughtered now," the narrator adds, "and I don't remember mine" (*HF*, 41). Both the woman and the child have in a sense lost their faces, the outward evidence of their identity. Similarly, the cat's face is "blank" (*HF*, 13) and the burned moth is headless. Rather than implying a confusion about one's identity, these references suggest the emptiness of self that prepares the spiritual initiate for the influx of Spirit. Like the burned moth's hollow body that becomes the conduit for

the wax that allows her to keep on burning, the narrator's emptiness prepares her for her divine artistic mission. "I am hollow," she proclaims early in
the book (*HF*, 24).

Part of this emptying process is the rejection of analytical thinking, also
implied by the imagery of headlessness. The narrator quotes the sixth-
century mystic Dionysius the Areopagite for the advice to "[a]bandon
everything. God despises ideas" (*HF*, 45). All our analyses count for nothing when it comes to a confrontation with the holy—"when the dazzling
dark breaks over the far slopes of time, then it's time to toss things, like our
reason, and our will" (*HF*, 62). This emptiness leaves the narrator completely receptive to God. She has in effect become like the nun, whose life is
utterly dedicated to the love and worship of God. Here the imagery of fire
takes on additional significance as the burning love of God. Again citing
Dionysius, Dillard draws a connection among the artist, the nun, and the
heavenly seraphs. The seraphs, according to Dionysius, are six-winged angels who love God so intensely, the narrator relates, that they are continually
bursting into flame as they sing his praise. Like the nun and the artist, they
are "aflame with love for God" (*HF*, 45).

Dillard's use of the nun as another image for the artist reinforces the
themes already introduced by her treatment of the moth, the child, and the
cat. At first the narrator describes the painful aspect of the nun's life, her
separation from human society. Like the narrator-artist, the nun is without
husband or child, and she is isolated from the mainstream of human society.
She too is "hollow," having given up her life and her individual identity to
dedicate her life to her spiritual mission. Fearing that the scarred Julie will
be rejected by society, the narrator tells her, "You might as well be a nun"
(*HF*, 74).

But the narrator quickly turns to the compensating blessings of the nun's
life: the power of her relationship with God. She tells the young Julie to
"learn power, the smash of the holy," which is so forceful that she "won't be
able to sleep, or need to, for the joy of it." She predicts, still addressing Julie,
that on some days this power will be so great that Julie will have to hold the
altar rail "so you won't fly" (*HF*, 75). Her sleepless nights will be filled with
visions and revelations: "You cry, My father, My father, the chariots of Israel, and the horsemen thereof! Held, held fast by love in the world like the
moth in wax, your life a wick, your head on fire with prayer, held utterly,
outside and in, you sleep alone, if you call that alone, you cry God" (*HF*,
75). Despite the sacrifice involved in a life of such dedication, the almost-
total union with God is a more than adequate reward. By the end of *Holy
the Firm*, the narrator has changed her tune. Julie will lead a normal life

someday, but the narrator will be the nun: "So live. I'll be the nun for you. I am now" (*HF*, 76).

Dillard's use of the name Julie Norwich for the child brings additional significance to the nun imagery. Julian of Norwich was a fourteenth-century English mystic, a Benedictine nun who wrote the Christian classic *Revelations of Divine Love*. Her book describes a series of visions she experienced during a serious illness in 1373. Dillard has stated that she had the courage to read the book only once (Yancey, 963), but its impact on her spiritual development is strongly evident in *Holy the Firm*. In a 1980 article in *Fourteenth Century English Mystics Newsletter* Jacob Gaskins identified many of Dillard's allusions to Julian's *Revelations of Divine Love* in *Holy the Firm*.[13] He shows that Dillard's language is often so similar to Julian's that the source of the allusion is unmistakable. In addition to language similarities, both writers emphasize the unfathomable love of God for mankind, both believe God is present in all things, and both sense he is the very "ground" of our being. While Julian does not address the specific problem of physical suffering, she does make it clear that God neither wishes nor causes suffering to man. She would certainly agree with Dillard's concluding premise: that the events of this world, even the most horrifying suffering, are insignificant compared with the joy of relationship with the living, loving God—a God who holds humankind fast in his infinite love.

Another image Dillard uses to illustrate the role of the artist is that of the prophet. This imagery is not introduced until part 3, nearly at the book's end, but it is an important aspect of the resolution of the crisis of faith that develops in part 2. Dillard quotes verbatim Isaiah 6:8, which relates the calling of Isaiah to the life of the prophet. In Isaiah's vision God, surrounded by the heavenly seraphs, asks, "Whom shall I send and who will go for us?" Significantly, Isaiah nominates himself. As Dillard explains it, "And poor Isaiah, who happened to be standing there—and there was no one else—burst out, 'Here am I, send me!'" (*HF*, 73). Dillard suggests that Isaiah volunteered not because he was more holy or pure than anyone else but because there was no one else to go.

The imagery of the prophet is particularly appropriate for describing the artist, since both the artist and the prophet are driven to share a vision they have received. The artist is not commanded to that role by God; rather, she makes a conscious decision to undertake it. An internal force—be it God or something else—compels her, like Isaiah, to step forward. She is no better than anyone else, no more holy, and no more pure. This is a frequent refrain of Dillard herself, who often complains that after reading her books readers expect her to be some kind of saint. In an interview shortly after the publication of *Holy the Firm* she tried to dispel those expectations with this comment: "I don't know anything about God, any more than anybody else does. . . . I'm just writing this book, and trying to turn your attention to God" (Burnett, 90). Just as the prophet is not necessarily perfect, Dillard is not perfect. But she is driven to share her vision, driven by the fear that if she does not do so, perhaps no one else will either, for as her narrator explains, "There is no one but us. . . . There never has been" (*HF*, 56). It will not do to look around to see who else can play the role.

Dillard also portrays the artist as Mary, the holy vessel who bore Christ into the world. Shortly before the narrator's vision of Christ's baptism, she describes carrying the communion wine in language suggestive of Mary's bearing of Christ: "I bear holiness splintered into a vessel, very God of very God, the sempiternal silence personal and brooding" (*HF*, 64). As the vision deepens, she feels light "filling the buttressed vaults of [her] ribs," as though she bore Christ himself within her body (*HF*, 65). Dillard's descriptions of the world entering the ear of the narrator may even be viewed as allusions to the medieval belief that Mary was impregnated by the Holy Spirit through her ear (*HF*, 12, 28).[14] In part 2, describing the view of faith, the narrator again uses the imagery of motherhood, concluding that God is "our baby to bear" (*HF*, 47). In the most profound sense, then, the work of the artist, the narrator concludes, brings God into the world, "pale and astounded" (*HF*, 71).

This imagery of mankind as the mother bearing the Christ child into the world through the pain of labor has an eminent antecedent in chapter 8 of the apostle Paul's letter to the Romans. In fact, that chapter may be viewed as a key to Dillard's theology in *Holy the Firm*. Paul writes that the whole creation, humanity included, "groaneth and travaileth in pain together until now" (Rom. 8:22). This chapter also contains Paul's eloquent response to the problem of apparently meaningless suffering, in terms that are reminiscent, again, of the views of Julian of Norwich. First, he reminds Christians of the immeasurable joy of a relationship with God: "For I reckon that the sufferings of this present time are not worthy to be compared with the glory which shall be revealed to us" (8:18). Second, he assures Christians of the workings of a divine albeit inscrutable plan: "And we know that all things work together for good to them that love God, to them who are the called according to his purpose" (8:28). Dillard concludes that these are the answers only faith can give—to questions that must otherwise remain unanswered.

Ultimately, the narrator-artist becomes both the bearer of Christ and Christ himself. The artist becomes the sacrificial lamb, whose metaphorical death helps lift the pain of life above the mundane and into the realm of the holy. The burning of her pain is the light that illuminates the world; her body and her work "span the gap" connecting time and eternity. In *Pilgrim* Dillard identified the alchemical Philosopher's Stone as the unification of heaven and earth. Here in *Holy the Firm* she refines that concept, identifying the Philosopher's Stone, which is "Holy the Firm," with the artist and her work. Early in part 3 the narrator states, "For me, there is, I am trying to tell you, no time" (*HF*, 68). Rather than a statement of the imminence of her death, this is a statement of the powerful effect of art: its ability to bring together the world of Spirit and the world of matter in a blinding moment of timelessness, a moment that drowns all questions in the flood of its silence and its peace.

Style in *Holy the Firm*

As always, reviewers were quick to praise Dillard's style in *Holy the Firm*, describing it as "mountain-flying prose" and "rarely less than superb."[15] "For sustained intensity," praised one, "her style is not easily matched anywhere in contemporary writing" (Buechner, 12). Unlike the lush, diffused density of *Pilgrim*, however, the language in *Holy the Firm* is sparse, concentrated, and precise. The result is a prose that is lean, controlled, and powerful. Dillard admits she had learned much during and after the writing of *Pilgrim*. In her essay explaining how she wrote the moth essay, she humbly confessed, "Actually, it took me about ten years to learn to write clearly. When I was in my twenties, I was more interested in showing off" ("How I Wrote," 19).

While it surpasses *Pilgrim* in clarity, *Holy the Firm* still retains the poetic quality that earned praise for *Pilgrim*. Reviewers have commented on Dillard's use of rhythm, metaphor, metonomy, synecdoche, alliteration, and other techniques associated with poetry. The form itself is also poetic; one reviewer, for example, viewed the book "as a kind of sestina with changes rung on words like salt, flame, holy, moth, and nun" (Buechner, 40). This poetic quality is partly due to the fact that *Holy the Firm* started out as a poem; shortly after writing the moth essay, Dillard decided to incorporate it into the book and put the entire work into a prose format (Yancey, 961; "How I Wrote," 20). But even after deciding to write the book as prose, she still intentionally structured it like poetry. Soon after writing *Holy the Firm*, she explained in an interview with Michael Burnett that she was "trying to expand the boundaries of non-fiction prose, so that the structures of poetry . . . obtain and work for that prose the way they do in the highly-intellectualized poetry of the last three centuries in the West." She stated that *Holy the Firm* was "more like a poem. . . . [I]t is just bristling with the kind of meaning that is poetry" (Burnett, 102).

The critics' praise of Dillard's poetic language shows that she did in fact succeed in compressing poetic meaning into the prose of *Holy the Firm*. Reviewer Mike Major phrased it this way: "In other words, her nonfiction doesn't simply explain meaning, but through its use of language, internal tensions and rhythms, becomes meaning. Dillard's nonfiction reads like poetry because, in fact, it is."[16] One practical effect of this technique is that it helps retain the impression of the ineffability of the spiritual encounter. Paradoxically, it also conveys a more forceful image of the nature of that encounter. Religious tradition leads us to expect one returning from an encounter with God to shine with radiance or sing and dance for joy; Dillard's poetic prose convincingly simulates both. In the words of the Roman Catholic theologian John Shea, "This is not another book about spirituality. It is a spirituality, a person seeing and breathing out of the experience of the living God."[17]

Dillard's use of the first-person point of view reinforces this impression that *Holy the Firm* is genuine spiritual autobiography. While critical readers must always beware of mistaking fictional personae for their authors, Dillard has admitted that she envisions the speaker in *Holy the Firm* as herself.[18] In fact, she has called it "the most personal" of all her books (Trueheart, 1; "How I Wrote," 21). Dillard explained to the interviewer Philip Yancey that when she originally planned the book, she decided in advance to write about whatever happened to her in the next three days. On the second day, the plane actually crashed. She described her response: "I thought, Oh no, God's making me write about this damn problem of pain again. I felt I was too young, I didn't know the answer and I didn't want to—but again, I had to" (Yancey, 959, 961). In the truest sense *Holy the Firm* is spiritual autobiography: it records Dillard's own personal spiritual struggles.

Chapter Five
Quit Your Tents—Pray without Ceasing

In 1982 Dillard released a collection of essays, *Teaching a Stone to Talk*, and her first book of literary criticism, *Living by Fiction*. Critics seemed to breathe a sigh of relief in their reviews of *Teaching a Stone to Talk*. Strongly reminiscent of *Pilgrim at Tinker Creek*, it was familiar ground after the disorienting profundity of *Holy the Firm*, and many reviewers saw it as harking back to her earlier work. In fact, many of the essays appearing in *Teaching a Stone to Talk* had been previously published, some as early as 1973—a year before *Pilgrim* was published and four years before *Holy the Firm* was published. Undeniably these essays belong to what might be called the early period of Dillard's writing career.

Readers notice, nevertheless, a critical difference between Dillard's previous two books of prose and the essays in *Teaching a Stone to Talk*. All three books evidence the characteristics that made *Pilgrim* a prizewinner for Dillard—her striking use of metaphor, the clarity and originality of her prose, her intensely precise powers of observation, and her mystical bent. The essays, however, are somewhat different in tone because in them Dillard is less introspective than in her previous books. This difference takes the form of an increase in the frequency and intensity of the narrator's interactions with other people. In almost every one of these 14 essays, people other than the narrator are present, and more often than not they are critically involved in the action and theme.

Critics seemed to view this increased human interaction as a new development in Dillard's career. One reviewer, for instance, rejoiced that the "sometimes intense individualism of her earlier books is complemented here by the presence of other people."[1] Another happily declared that Dillard was "now more convincingly a humanist."[2] These sentiments result in large part from a misunderstanding of Dillard, whose interest in other people should never have been in question. All her books before *Teaching a Stone to Talk*, including *Tickets for a Prayer Wheel*, reflect her great concern for and love of people—most specifically in her preoccupation with suffering, pain, and death. This sensitivity takes especially poignant form in her expressions of grief for the burned child Julie in *Holy the Firm*. These concerns are also apparent in her book of poems, in which she clearly throws her lot in with that of the rest of humanity, and in her occasional short stories.

In *Pilgrim* the relative infrequency of human interaction resulted from Dillard's use of the "disembodied eyeball" viewpoint of Emerson and Thoreau. Readers not recognizing this technique sometimes concluded that Dillard was out of touch with the mainstream of human affairs. The tendency of interviewers, as well as promoters of her books, to portray her as almost reclusive helped spread this misconception. The result was a cult of personality that envisioned Dillard as a spiritual hermit, a kind of sprite who frequented wild and isolated places.

In her 1978 interview with Philip Yancey, Dillard got the opportunity to set the record straight. When asked why she wrote so rarely about people, seemingly more fascinated by objects and nature, she responded that people did fascinate her just as much. She added, "I just don't think I'm good enough to write about people yet. I'd love to try some day."[3] Thus, the so-called intense individualism of *Pilgrim* indicated more than anything else a deep sense of humility about her own skills. Dillard's release of the essays in *Teaching a Stone to Talk* shows her increased confidence. While in *Pilgrim* she worked hard to create the illusion of her isolation in the apparent wilderness of the Roanoke Valley, in *Teaching a Stone to Talk* she openly admits that the same geographical area is far from being an isolated wilderness. In "Living Like Weasels" she confides, "This is, mind you, suburbia."[4] *Teaching a Stone to Talk* is Dillard's statement that she is ready to write about people, and for the reader it has been well worth the wait. In the words of Virginia Stem Owens, "There are people in her latest book and they are indeed overwhelming."[5]

The 14 essays in *Teaching a Stone to Talk* bear the mark of the author's final spit and polish. Like many writers, Dillard often continues to modify and rewrite her works long after they first appear in print. She has confessed, for example, that she continued to revise the essay "Lenses" for seven years after she first recorded the incident in her journal. Still, she considered it "easy" to write, requiring "only" six or seven versions, although she admitted to being not completely satisfied with it even then.[6] Her perfectionism and the tendency to continually revise her work virtually assured the excellence of the essays in *Teaching a Stone to Talk*. Her effort on these pieces did not go unnoticed. Reviewers labeled the book "a series of meticulously crafted essays" and "a collection of meditations like polished stones."[7] "The book is eccentric, passionate, and brilliant," another declared.[8] With very few exceptions, critics highly praised Dillard's work in *Teaching a Stone to*

Talk, finding it a worthy successor to *Pilgrim at Tinker Creek* and *Holy the Firm*.

An Overview of *Teaching a Stone to Talk*

Like the poems in *Tickets for a Prayer Wheel*, the essays in *Teaching a Stone to Talk* vary greatly in format and subject. In length the 14 essays range from a mere 3 pages in "God in the Doorway" to 35 pages in "An Expedition to the Pole." Ten of the essays are moderately short, 5 to 10 pages. Four others, including "Expedition to the Pole," are 20 to 35 pages. All are written in the first person, in a genre Virginia Stem Owens has labeled "storified nonfiction," or "testimony" (Owens, 24). Although Owens acknowledges that the essays in *Teaching a Stone to Talk* "are not, generically speaking, fiction," they are nonetheless stories, and Owens sees in Dillard "one of the best practitioners [of storytelling] of our time" (Owens, 23). Owens praises Dillard for successfully avoiding the dangers of using herself and her life as her main subject and discusses Dillard's career as a progressive development of this new genre of "storified nonfiction."

The essays in *Teaching a Stone to Talk* also range broadly in what might be called "setting"—that is, the location of the incident in Dillard's life that serves as the focal point for each essay. The majority of the essays revolve around incidents that occurred in or near her home when she lived in the Roanoke Valley in Virginia and on Puget Sound in Washington. "On a Hill Far Away," for instance, takes place in the same area near Tinker Creek that provided the stage for *Pilgrim at Tinker Creek*. "Mirages" describes the view from the cabin in which she wrote *Holy the Firm*. Two essays recall experiences from Dillard's childhood in Pittsburgh, "God in the Doorway" and "Lenses." Another describes a weekend visit with a young child—to a cabin in an undesignated area in the Appalachian mountains. Three of the essays relate Dillard's experiences when she traveled with three other journalists in Ecuador and the Galapagos Islands: "In the Jungle," "The Deer at Providencia," and "Life on the Rocks: The Galapagos."

As far as subject is concerned, the essays are equally diverse. The following brief synopses provide an overview of the collection.

In "Living Like Weasels," Dillard describes her encounter with a weasel, an animal notorious for its tenacity in dealing with enemies. Using the weasel's tenacity as a metaphor, she exhorts the reader to live like a weasel, pursuing and grasping our "one necessity" and not letting it go.

"An Expedition to the Pole" is the critics' favorite of the collection, described as "brilliantly constructed" and "one of the book's most innovative and profound pieces."[9] In it Dillard discusses the folly of inadequately prepared polar explorers of the nineteenth century and compares that folly with comic attempts of man to seek God in a Roman Catholic worship service she has attended.

"In the Jungle" is an easygoing description of Dillard's visit to a peaceful village on the Napo River in the Ecuadorian jungle. Its heavenly ambience reflects a theme of paradise lost and regained that runs through the essays in *Teaching a Stone to Talk*. In "The Deer at Providencia" Dillard describes the suffering of a deer being "prepared" for a meal by natives at another village on the Napo River. To tenderize the meat, the deer has been tied in such a way that it will slowly and painfully struggle itself to death. Dillard uses the incident as an opportunity to comment on the proper response to what she calls the "mystery" of suffering.

In "Teaching a Stone to Talk," the title essay, Dillard tells of the allegedly real-life attempts of a neighbor to teach a stone to talk. She relates this mission to mankind's desire to hear God's voice in the silence of nature. "On a Hill Far Away" describes the narrator's poignant encounter with a young boy whose fundamental Christianity requires him to ask all strangers whether they have been saved. Dillard expresses admiration for the courage of such Christian witnesses but implies that in her mind true witness requires a different sort of conduct.

"Total Eclipse" is another favorite of reviewers and critics. In it Dillard describes a total eclipse of the sun that she and her husband viewed in 1979. The dramatic experience evokes in its viewers irrational emotions, ones Dillard compares with dying, traveling backward in time, and descending into a primitive mode of consciousness.

In "Lenses" Dillard compares her childhood viewing of a drop of pond water under a microscope with her adulthood viewing, through binoculars, of swans winging through the sky above a pond. She uses the drying and death of the organisms under the microscope's light to evoke the sense of an impending apocalypse of the larger world. The effect is to convey a sense of human vulnerability and mortality.

In "Life on the Rocks: The Galapagos" Dillard describes her visit to the Galapagos Islands, emphasizing the lack of fear of the wildlife toward people or toward other species on the islands. She describes this idyllic interaction in terms that again suggest an Eden-like paradise at the beginning of time, and makes the point that all organisms are interconnected in the intricate web of creation.

"A Field of Silence" is an enigmatic piece that describes Dillard's perception of holiness on a farm where she lived in the Puget Sound area. The holiness appears to her as the silence of God in the form of a palpable presence, not unlike the presence of angels. This presence, however, although divine, is paradoxically melancholy, suggesting a sense of isolation and loneliness. While she feels that the perception is revelatory in nature, she consciously rejects its vision and "breaks the spell."

In "God in the Doorway" Dillard writes of her childhood fear of Santa Claus and compares it with her continuing fear of God. She tells of a friendly neighbor, Miss White, who, dressed as Santa, surprised and frightened the young Dillard. She realized much later that the woman meant only love, just as God means only love, and she remorsefully concludes that the human tendency is to run from God just as she ran from Miss White.

"Mirages" appears on the surface to be merely a description of mirages that Dillard studied through binoculars when she lived on Puget Sound. A closer look, however, reveals the essay to be a meditation on the nature of reality and the illusion of appearances.

In "Sojourner" Dillard describes the fragile existence of the tropical mangrove tree, which can live afloat in the saltwater of the ocean by accumulating dirt and debris around its roots. She compares the mangrove to the human race, isolated and afloat in hostile space. It miraculously survives, she surmises, through the accumulated "muck of soil" around its roots—the unifying force of human culture.

"Aces and Eights," another favorite of the critics, describes Dillard's weekend visit to a woodland cabin with a nine-year-old child. It is a masterpiece of nostalgia, an essay in which Dillard contrasts youth with age, past with present, and experience with memory. The result is a bittersweet reflection on the effects of time on human consciousness and relationship.

Teaching a Stone to Talk can be characterized as a thoughtful meditation on the human condition. In this sense it is the most existential of all Dillard's books, although clearly it is Christian existentialism she embraces. In this book Dillard takes an honest look at what it means to be a human being alive on earth, freely embracing all the suffering and joy such a life entails. Her response to the inevitable suffering of life is the response of faith, but it is neither naive nor unrealistic. It is above all a courageous faith, reflecting the willingness to think even the unthinkable—that perhaps life is, after all, meaningless.

The Human Condition

In *Teaching a Stone to Talk* as in all her books, Dillard puzzles over and rebels against the cruel overlord of time. The reviewer Christopher Lehmann-Haupt goes so far as to say that "this is what . . . 'Teaching a Stone to Talk' is about—the fall into nature and relentless time."[10] The book contains many striking metaphors to describe this relentlessness of time and its brutal, impersonal effects on the earth and its inhabitants. In "Life on the Rocks," for example, as in previous works, Dillard uses the familiar imagery of the ice age to illustrate the ravages of time on the earth. "The ice rolled up, the ice rolled back," she comments with feigned matter-of-factness (*TST*, 111). In "Aces and Eights," on the other hand, she describes time as a moving train. Jumping from it at high speed is a risky business, she cautions, despite tongue-in-cheek instructions for how to do so safely.

Another, and certainly the central, image for time in "Aces and Eights," however, is the clicking of playing cards clipped with clothespins to the child's bicycle wheels. Almost humorously illustrating the sentiment behind the phrase "over the hill," the clicking gradually speeds up as the child rides down a steep hill. The metaphor is made even more pointed because the child has chosen pairs of aces and eights to attach to her bike—the "dead man's hand," as the narrator had explained to the child during a game of poker the evening before. The speeding up of the clicking as the bike nears the bottom of the hill perfectly simulates the perception of time's increasing speed as old age approaches. Eventually the clicking is so fast that it resembles, in the narrator's mind, the whine of bombs bearing certain destruction and death. This imagery of the passage of time as clicking—obviously suggestive of the ticking of a clock or a time bomb—brings to mind the clicking Dillard described in part 1 of *Holy the Firm*, which also involves the fall into time.

In *Teaching a Stone to Talk* as in *Holy the Firm*, Dillard associates the fall into time first and foremost with the certainty of human mortality. While Dillard rarely directly discusses death in these essays, it often appears thinly veiled in chilling metaphors. In "Lenses" it takes the form of an implied apocalypse as the whole natural world is metaphorically transformed into a drop of water that is shrinking toward annihilation. In "Life on the Rocks" the termination of tracks where birds flew into the sky prompts the narrator to reflect on death, "Our tracks do that: but we go down. And stay down" (*TST*, 115). In "Aces and Eights" human mortality is suggested by the burning candles the narrator and child watch float down the river until they burn out. It also takes the form of a blast of cold wind from the North that portends the coming of fall and, after it, winter.

In "Eclipse" the irrational fear inspired by a view of the partial eclipse of the sun becomes another powerful metaphor for the fear of death. Dillard ascribes the fear, which seems to border on hysteria, to the wall of darkness that appears to rush toward viewers as the cone of the moon's darkness moves across the sun, and to the unearthly light that illuminates the world when the sun is covered. "It had been like dying," Dillard begins the essay (*TST*, 84). Later she prays the reader "will never see anything more awful in the sky" (*TST*, 95). The experience evokes strongly primitive emotions that connect the narrator to mankind at the beginning of time.

Another aspect of the human condition Dillard confronts in *Teaching a Stone to Talk* is the inevitability of suffering. In "The Deer at Providencia" she probes this subject with remarkable restraint and sensitivity. After describing the struggles of the dying deer, she turns to human suffering in terms reminiscent of *Holy the Firm*. She relates the story of a man badly burned for the second time in his life—ironically, after undergoing 13 years of operations to repair damage caused by an earlier burn. She had been so moved by the story, she tells her reader, that she taped the newspaper article about the incident to her bedroom mirror, forcing herself to read it every morning. She is justifiably disturbed by the incident, as she surely is also disturbed by the sufferings of the deer. But she seems to maintain that the proper response to suffering is not maudlin pity but rather respectful silence. "These things are not issues," she declares. "They are mysteries" (*TST*, 63).

The pain of loss is another truth Dillard explores in these essays. She does so masterfully in "Aces and Eights," which Virginia Stem Owens describes as gradually building to a "sense of bereavement, the elemental loss no time-bound creature can escape" (Owens, 25). Despite the inescapability of such pain, the narrator tells the reader that she did halfheartedly try to escape it. Knowing from the start that spending the weekend with the child would cause her pain, she tried to talk herself into staying home. In the essay's beginning line she confides, "I am here against my good judgment" (*TST*, 153). By the story's end her surrender seems as inevitable as the ubiquity of loss itself.

Dillard's refusal to identify the child in "Aces and Eights"—most likely one of her stepdaughters from her first marriage—helps make the sense of loss more universal. The child in effect becomes the symbol of all things once dear and treasured but now lost. The power of specificity is not sacrificed through this technique. In Dillard's capable hands the child becomes a very real person who grows irretrievably into the heart of the reader. That these two persons are permitted only brief encounters such as this weekend makes their bittersweet relationship all the more precious. As the narrator sums it up, "We have lived together so often, and parted so many times, that the very sight of each other means loss" (*TST*, 156). In this essay, which more than any of the others deserves the label story, Dillard has outdone herself in weaving beauty and pain into one seamless whole.

But in "Aces and Eights" Dillard does not stop at portraying the loss of loved ones; she also tackles the loss of each person's own past and all that such a loss entails: lost dreams, lost goals, lost innocence, lost beliefs. The narrator describes her own childhood and the vows she had made to herself—always to love a certain boy, always to hate her sister and to hate playing the piano, and never to change as everyone assured her she would. As a child, and even now as an adult, she saw these changes as so profound that they constituted a betrayal of the self, even a kind of suicide that she "was being borne helplessly" toward (*TST*, 163). The narrator is forced to watch these changes, which she still mourns in her own life, as they inexorably transform the child, who bit by bit is herself becoming aware, as Dillard phrases it, "of some of the losses you incur by being here" (*TST*, 156).

This sense of loss from continual change is another facet of the human condition that Dillard presents in *Teaching a Stone to Talk*. The awareness of change in the past makes individuals more self-conscious in the present. For example, in "Aces and Eights" the narrator catches the child imagining herself in the future, grown and married with four children. That glimpse into the future in turn causes the child to look at the narrator with new eyes, viewing her as one who also was once a child and who has now grown into the woman before her. The narrator's awareness of her own lost childhood, on the other hand, causes her to see her own past in the child and to look with nostalgic sadness on the child's future. Dillard illustrates this truth with a telling description of the child looking at her reflection in a window. Inside her own reflected outline the child sees a smaller reflection of the narrator, a unique portrayal of her future adult self contained within her present child self. With these inner reflections on self and other, Dillard shows how the past, present, and future reverberate with each other's presence, each reflecting and changing the other.

Dillard describes another aspect of this self-consciousness in her portrayal of the process of memory construction. Throughout the weekend visit, the narrator analyzes the present moment for how well it will play back as a memory. While watching the candles float down the stream, she complains that the experience should somehow be better, but concludes, "As a memory, however, it is already looking good" (*TST,* 160). Critical yet tolerant of her own human nature, she comments on the predictable idealization of the past that takes place in the human mind. She admits that the death of the old man Noah Very, for instance, makes her recall him more fondly than he deserved. While she disdains what she describes at the essay's beginning as "some absurd, manufactured nostalgia" (*TST,* 154), by the end of the essay she has given in to this inevitable process of idealized memory construction. Dillard implies that the intense and multiple reality of the actual moment is too full for words or memory to capture. The idealization is perhaps a consolation for what is lost. She describes this unexpected uniqueness of the present moment as she and the child take one last look before leaving the cabin: "We are, alas, imagining ourselves in the future remembering standing here now, the morning light on the green valley and on the clear river, the child playing with the woman's fingers. I had not thought of that before we came, that she would be playing with my fingers, or that we would hear trucks shifting down to climb the hill behind the cottage" (*TST,* 177).

In *Teaching a Stone to Talk* Dillard presents loneliness as another inevitable life experience. One type of loneliness she describes is the simple feeling that results from being physically alone. In the essay "On a Hill Far Away" she illustrates this type of loneliness in her depiction of the young Christian boy who has no one to play with. His loneliness is so painfully obvious that it prompts the narrator to recall her own childhood, thanking God for the sisters and friends that kept her from such a fate. She also describes the loneliness of the boy's mother, who is isolated from mainstream society by her fundamentalist views. Dillard feels no animosity toward such fundamentalists and in fact admires their devotion to God. When asked by the boy's mother whether she "knows the Lord" as her "personal savior," the narrator comments that "[m]y heart went out to her" (*TST,* 80). Although the narrator does respond that she knows the Lord, the chasm between the life-styles and the views of the two women remains great.

Dillard uses many different images in *Teaching a Stone to Talk* to illustrate the separateness of mankind from God. One recurring image is that of mankind drifting like an island. In "Sojourners," for instance, the floating mangrove tree becomes a metaphor for the human race on the earth, which drifts through space separate and alone. Dillard describes earth as "a sojourner in airless space, a wet ball flung across nowhere" (*TST,* 151). As in *Pilgrim at Tinker Creek,* she comments on the seeming alienness of this planet and wonders how it can possibly be humankind's "home." In "Life on the Rocks" she again uses the imagery of floating to suggest this aloneness. Speaking of the continents, she reminds the reader that "[w]e're on floating islands, shaky ground" (*TST*, 129), and once again she speaks of humankind—using biblical language—as both stranger and sojourner in an alien land. A strong sense of vulnerability and directionlessness exists in the imagery of floating she employs. We have been left "exposed, and drifting," she observes in a tone both courageous and melancholy (*TST*, 123).

Dillard uses the silence of nature as another metaphor for the separation between God and humankind. The title essay, "Teaching a Stone to Talk," directly addresses the issue of the silence of nature—which she takes to be the silence of God. Her neighbor Larry's attempts to teach a stone to talk represent the noble attempts of humankind to communicate with God. Just as Larry's efforts to get a word out of his stone are futile, so humankind's efforts to force a word out of God are futile. "Nature's silence is its one remark," she reiterates (*TST*, 69), cautioning those who seek God not to expect a response. This refusal of God to respond, this silence, separates God from humanity as well as humanity from God. In "A Field of Silence" Dillard describes the silence of God lying heavy on the land as "loneliness unendurable" (*TST*, 137). It evokes in the narrator strong feelings of sorrow—the sorrow of the separation of humanity from God and the ensuing loneliness of both humanity and God.

In the essay "Teaching a Stone to Talk" Dillard provides a legendary explanation for God's silence. In Deuteronomy, she relates, the Israelites told Moses to beg God not to speak to them directly because his presence, full of thundering and smoking, frightened them. According to this story, she implies, it was humanity's choice to be free from the presence and the voice of God. As Dillard concludes, "We doused the burning bush and cannot rekindle it" (*TST*, 70). Dillard tells this biblical story to show that fear is at the root of humankind's separation from God. In this context the response of the viewers of the solar eclipse described in "Eclipse" becomes a metaphor for humanity's fear of the presence of God. The narrator reports that as soon as the full eclipse is over, the many viewers on the hillside, including her and her husband, quickly got in their cars and left, even though a remarkable view of the partial eclipse was still visible. The narrator's explanation is that "[o]ne turns at last even from glory itself with a sigh of relief" (*TST*, 103).

Dillard illustrates this ambivalence toward God in her essay "God in the Doorway," which relates her childish fear of Santa Claus. The parallel between God and Santa Claus is clear; both are omnipotent and omniscient, and both know "who's been bad or good." The reason for the young narrator's fear of Santa is also obvious: she had, at least in her own mind, been bad. That explains the child's fear when the well-meaning Miss White came to the door dressed as Santa Claus. Dillard uses the child's running from Miss White as a unique metaphor for man's mistaken fear of and running from the love of God. Such fear results from guilty self-knowledge and from the failure to believe in a love great enough to forgive what we cannot forgive in ourselves. It is this self-hatred that drives humankind from God. It creates the expectation, and perhaps even the desire, of punishment, projecting on God its own motives of self-abasement.

"In God in the Doorway" God, in the guise of Santa Claus, stands in the doorway of the narrator's home—an image implying the readiness of God to enter each life, bearing only love and acceptance. This image reverses the notion contained in the Gospels of man's need to knock at God's door to receive spiritual life; rather, it is God himself who knocks at each door, and each individual need only open the door and allow God to enter. The fear of God that Dillard depicts in "God in the Doorway" is, she implies, the only force separating humanity from God. But it is a powerful force, one that has kept humanity from God throughout history. She concludes the essay with a strong statement of humanity's mistaken fear and rejection of the love of God: "So once in Israel love came to us incarnate, stood in the doorway between two worlds, and we were all afraid" (*TST*, 141).

Overall, Dillard portrays the human condition as a test of endurance, a trial by fire. Humankind is held in the clutches of time, subject to the ravages of aging, illness, and death. In a lifetime each individual will inevitably experience pain, heartbreak, loss, and grief, along with personal changes so profound as to amount to betrayal and death of the self. At one time or another, all will also experience the pain of loneliness and alienation from others. The great tragedy is that human nature itself seems to forbid spiritual comfort during these trials, for humankind inevitably runs from the God who alone can offer enduring support and love. This, then, is the world in which we find ourselves, and the world to which we must somehow forge a response.

Forging a Response to the Human Condition

Dillard's intellectual honesty forces her to concede that life may indeed be meaningless. Her response to that possibility, however, is not despair. In "Sojourners" she concludes, "Even if things are as bad as they could possibly be, and as meaningless, then matters of truth are themselves indifferent; we may as well please our sensibilities and, with as much spirit as we can muster, go out with a buck and wing" (*TST*, 152). After all, Dillard reminds her readers, meaning is itself a human concept—as is meaninglessness. She illustrates this point in "Eclipse." The principal cause of horror among those viewing the eclipse, she shows, is the confrontation with their own insignificance. Any meaning they attach to their lives is of their own making. "For what is significance?" she questions. "It is significance for people. No people, no significance" (*TST*, 94).

Dillard intimates that humankind must somehow lift itself by its own bootstraps and, if necessary, create its own meaning. Throughout *Teaching a Stone to Talk*, she hints that this is exactly what humankind has always done, creating its own reality by conscious or unconscious choice. For example, she often uses imagery of lenses—microscopes, binoculars, and magnifying glasses—to show that viewpoint and expectation influence and even create experience. Her essay "Mirages" is a study of this process of the creation of experience. She views mirages on the water of Puget Sound through binoculars and finds that the closer she looks, the more real they appear. She explains that the brain, expecting to see the usual, fills in the necessary gaps so that no inconsistency appears. The meaning the human mind sees in life, she seems to suggest, is like the mirages; the brain fills in the gaps. Life is full of mirages, she tells the reader: "We live in a hall of mirrors rimmed by a horizon holey and warped" (*TST*, 144).

Faced, then, with the choice of creating meaning, each individual must decide what meaning to create in life and thereby lift himself or herself out of the pit of insignificance. Dillard does not abandon her readers to struggle alone through this process; she has her own ideas about the desirability of various belief systems and does not hesitate to promulgate them in *Teaching a Stone to Talk*. In this regard her essays present a body of precepts similar to those contained in *Pilgrim at Tinker Creek* and summarized in chapter 2 of this book. Here, however, she is more in the mainstream of twentieth-century philosophical and intellectual thought. Although her position still is based on her personal mystical experience of the presence of God, the strength of her argument does not depend on those mystical elements. The system of belief she commends to the reader does not require experience of the mystical union and is thus able to appeal to believer and nonbeliever alike.

Perhaps the most important component of the belief system Dillard presents, and the one that forms the basis for the other components, is the conviction that a web of relationship connects all creation. This web of life is not static but, rather, consists of continual change. Dillard shows that the living creatures and even the nonliving objects of the world take part in an unceasing give-and-take. As she explains in "Life on the Rocks: The Galapagos," "the rocks shape life, and then life shapes life, [and then] life shapes the rocks" (*TST*, 129). Past, present, and future time are connected in this view. This interconnectedness of time is behind Dillard's description of a rooster in "A Field of Silence" as reptilian, and her comparison of flying birds in "Aces and Eights" with lizards crawling on a ceiling (134, 166). The past continues to live in the present, she implies, just as the present will continue to live in the future.

The idea of a web of connection between all things becomes particularly significant in the context of human society. Just as living things interact with and change one another and their environment, so the individuals in human society take part in a dynamic process of movement and change. Here the complex interplay is between the extremes of communion and isolation. In the essays in *Teaching a Stone to Talk* Dillard shows that individuality develops in isolation but society develops in communion. Both elements are a necessary part of the human experience and are required for an individual to be fully human; any attempt to avoid the difficulty of human interaction must end in emptiness and futility. It is thus the coming together after separation that is the most significant human moment—and perhaps even the moment when humankind is at its most human.

These moments of coming together are portrayed with great poignancy in Dillard's essays. Although they smack of the ordinary, they are windows on the eternal, reflecting the truth of the universal. One such moment is the meeting between Dillard and the lonely young fundamentalist boy in the essay "On a Hill Far Away." Another is the narrator's encounter with five Ecuadorean children in a jungle village, all of whom insist on braiding her hair at the same time, "all fifty fingers," as Dillard describes it (*TST*, 54). Perhaps the best of these moments—and the capstone of the collection—is the coming together in "Aces and Eights," with its bittersweet visit between the narrator and the nine-year-old child she loves so dearly. That all these encounters involve children is surely no coincidence. It is in meetings between adults and children, after all, that past, present, and future come together most forcefully, and when so much is shared between human beings. It is in such meetings that adults realize what a thing to be treasured was their own innocence and youth, which they once bore so carelessly. It is in such moments that we all grow, finally, to treasure the gift of life with every last ounce of our being.

This is the stuff of which life's meaning is made, Dillard is saying in *Teaching a Stone to Talk*. It grows into a web from all life's little moments of love, pain, joy, and loneliness. The metaphor of the floating mangrove tree described in "Sojourner" aptly illustrates how this little appearing act is done. The mangrove floats in the poisonous saltwater of the ocean, alone and vulnerable just as mankind floats through space on the earth. Through chance encounters in the vastness of the open sea, the mangrove slowly accumulates debris in its roots. The debris develops into an entire ecosystem—a community—complete with freshwater, as well as other plants and living organisms. As Dillard explains at the essay's end, the human race is like the mangrove: it started out small and alone but has "accumulated a great and solacing muck of soil, of human culture" (*TST*, 152). The "muck" of human culture is thus the something-from-nothing that has bootstrapped human significance into existence. The development of human relationship—even if originally chance and meaningless—has in effect created its own meaning. This development, like that of the mangrove island, "turns drift to dance," creating direction, purpose, and beauty where before there was none (*TST*, 152).

From the view that human relationship creates its own meaning ex nihilo, it is but a short step to the conclusion that the individual who throws himself or herself into the human melee will experience greater richness and meaning in life. With this idea in mind Dillard points out the role of sacrifice, commitment, and dedication to others. More than acceptance of any religious dogma, it is involvement with others that creates man's salvation. Seeking to take the narrator's spiritual pulse, the young boy in the essay "On a Hill Far Away" asks the narrator, "Do you know the Lord as your personal savior?" She responds, "Not only that. I know your mother" (*TST*, 79). The implication is that knowing the boy's mother is one better than just knowing the Lord. Thus, Dillard suggests that relationships with people enrich and perhaps even constitute relationship with God.

Ironically, in *Teaching a Stone to Talk* Dillard—well known for her Christian mysticism—has pointed a way to reach God that de-emphasizes God. Abandoning the self to the love of others is the way to give life meaning and purpose, she exhorts. Surrendering to the human experience, with all its heartache and suffering, is the path to beauty and joy. She only hints that something unsought might be gained along the way, that God himself might be met in those moments of love and surrender. Here is an approach with more appeal to twentieth-century agnostics and existentialists than any contemporary mainstream religion can offer, an approach that leads readers to God through the back door and to heaven from the ground up. In the end, *Teaching a Stone to Talk* is about creating a response to God.

Forging a Response to God

In "An Expedition to the Pole" Dillard describes the comical lightheartedness with which members of the human society approach the worship of God. Some of these illustrations appear to be taken from Dillard's actual experiences in various church services during her life. She relates, for example, the nonchalant response of a teenager during the ritual of the "passing of the peace." He answers her greeting "Peace be with you" with a bored "Yeah." Similarly, she describes the incongruous clothing of a baby waiting to be baptized: his lace gown, blue tennis shoes, and red socks are an assault on the formality and solemnity of the occasion. Dillard also describes a bungled ecumenical service she attended, at which the priest and the minister whispered urgent questions to each other during the service. In contrast to all these she describes the serious attitude of eighteenth-century Hasidic Jews, who feared each prayer might be their last. She comments that in general she does not find Christians "sufficiently sensible" of the greatness of power that is invoked by the worship of God (*TST*, 40).

While she acknowledges infrequent exceptions, such as the Hasidim, Dillard portrays humanity overall as a laughingstock, a ship of fools—"cheerful, brainless tourists on a packaged tour of the Absolute" (*TST*, 40). The group with whom the narrator approaches the Pole is a perfect example. It consists of a troupe of circus clowns wearing crucifixes, a group of penguins, Admiral Peary and several other long-deceased polar explorers, the Filipino godfather of the child awaiting baptism, a country-and-western singer, two teenagers playing Frisbee, and a folksinging group. The narrator herself is dressed as a Keystone cop, beating a tambourine and singing "On Top of Old Smoky" to the accompaniment of a piano. Dillard's message seems to be that despite our best efforts, we are all clowns when it comes to approaching the Holy.

Dillard implies that man's inevitable absurdity cannot be masked by false attempts at dignity. To illustrate, she attributes the failure of early polar explorers largely to their foolish attempts to retain their dignity in the face of unimaginably harsh and alien conditions. The Franklin expedition of 1845, Dillard explains, took along such luxuries as sterling silver tableware with the family crests of the ship's officers but failed to take adequate coal or cold-weather clothing. Dillard reports that the frozen bodies of these men were later found scattered all over the polar region, often ludicrously carrying silverware or other "treasures." Dillard treats these luxuries as a metaphor for the emotional baggage holding man back from reaching God. She describes the "failed impersonations of human dignity" that people find so adorable in penguins, and she nervously wonders whether God will find man's impersonations of human dignity as endearing (*TST*, 42).

Dillard answers her own question with the reassurance that God's response to man's absurdity is indeed love and acceptance. The miracle, Dillard proclaims early in the essay, is "that God is so mighty he can stifle his own laughter" (*TST*, 20). At the end of the essay, in the midst of its surrealistic depiction of the approach to the Pole, she describes Christ crouched down and posing for snapshots "under the illusion" that all the people on the ice floe are penguins (*TST*, 52). His behavior shows not rejection but, rather, a lighthearted, affectionate acceptance of the absurdity of humankind. Dillard presents this acceptance of humanity as the main message of Christ's coming to earth. It is an unbelievable message: "Week after week Christ washes the disciples' dirty feet, handles their very toes, and repeats, It is all right—believe it or not—to be people. Who can believe it?" (*TST*, 20). The allusion is to John 15:3–8, in which Christ washes his disciples' feet. But the suggestion of continuing and repeated action in the present implies that the feet being washed are those of Christ's disciples today, perhaps even those of Dillard's readers themselves.

If one thing is clear in *Teaching a Stone to Talk*, it is that the salvation of the individual requires involvement with and commitment to other people. "There is no such thing as a solitary polar explorer," Dillard reminds her readers in "An Expedition to the Pole" (*TST*, 27). Consequently, in her own march to the "Pole of Relative Inaccessibility" she throws her lot in with the common people, comical and absurd as they may appear. This alliance requires total acceptance of one's own humanity as well as that of others; only acceptance and forgiveness of our own and others' humanity will allow us to receive Christ. In this context, then, acceptance of the humanity of Christ takes on added significance in that it requires the embracing of our own humanity as well.

Dillard's identification of God with man is, of course, embodied metaphorically and literally in the Christian doctrine of the dual nature of Christ. Dillard goes further than many mainstream Christians, however, by seeing God in all humankind, not just in Christ. This identity illuminates the nature of love of and service to one's fellow man: God is loved and served when man is loved and served. Dillard might even argue that God can be loved and served in no other way. Thus, her reference to Christ's washing of the disciples' feet in "An Expedition to the Pole" also illustrates Christ's exhortation to love and serve others, reflecting his words in Matthew 25:40: "Inasmuch as ye have done it unto one of the least of these my brethren, ye have done it unto me."

In addition to love and service, a willingness to sacrifice is part of the proper response to God. This willingness refers not to the sacrifice of material possessions but to the sacrifice of self. In "Teaching a Stone to Talk" Dillard assumes that the ritual her neighbor goes through to teach his stone to talk must involve "the suppression of self-consciousness . . . so that the will becomes transparent and hollow, a channel for the work" (*TST*, 68). This is no new idea for Dillard. In both *Pilgrim at Tinker Creek* and *Holy the Firm* she describes the emptying of the self that must take place before God can enter—the process of the *via negativa*. This process requires that we die to the self and, as Dillard describes it in "An Expedition to the Pole," that "we lose ourselves and turn from all that is not [God]" (*TST*, 31). Thus, when the offering plate is passed in church, the narrator throws in everything. Taking the symbolic role of a polar explorer, she refuses to make the mistakes of others before her by retaining her useless false dignity. She tosses in her schooling, her rank in the Royal Navy, her erroneous and incomplete charts, and more. All her beliefs about who and what she is must be jettisoned if she is to reach the point where "love for its own sake, lacking an object, begins" (*TST*, 48).

At this moment of absolute surrender of the self, all dialogue ceases, since there are no subject and object to take part in dialogue. There is, in fact, no self remaining to speak or to hear. "There is nothing to see or to know," the narrator intones in "An Expedition to the Pole." "My name is Silence" (*TST*, 48–49). This perception of God and self as absolute silence is described by Dillard as "a hum, a single chorused note everywhere the same" (*TST*, 72). At this point of enlightenment—when, ironically, there is no longer a self to "be" enlightened—the silence of nature and of God appears miraculously transformed. What human reason once perceived as meaningless nothingness becomes, from the spiritual "viewpoint," a something so complete and full that it is utterly beyond the human concept of meaning. Dillard concludes the essay "Teaching a Stone to Talk" with the realization of this silent fullness: "The silence is all there is. It is the alpha and the omega. It is God's brooding over the face of the waters; it is the blended note of ten thousand things, the whine of wings. You take a step in the right direction to pray to this silence, and even to address the prayer to 'World.' Distinctions blur. Quit your tents. Pray without ceasing" (76).

Thus, the final response to God must be silence. The prayer Dillard recommends in the foregoing passage is not the noisy prayer of the false self full of its own concerns; rather, it is prayer coming from the silence of self that meets the silence of God. The blurring of distinctions Dillard refers to is the oneness of God and human that occurs when the self is emptied.

"Quit your tents" is Dillard's response to the story in Deuteronomy of the Israelites begging God to be silent. It is her way of telling her reader to go back out into the world and find God there, hearing him in the silence that is his voice—rather than listening for him in words that fill the mistaken expectations of humanity's reasoning intellect.

Dillard speaks much about witnessing in *Teaching a Stone to Talk*. In the essay "On a Hill Far Away" she describes the painfully earnest efforts of the fundamentalist family to witness in their own way. They placed an eight-foot aluminum cross in their front yard along with a sign proclaiming "CHRIST THE LORD IS OUR SALVATION" (*TST*, 79). They also felt compelled to question every stranger they met about his or her personal salvation. While Dillard is tolerant of and even sympathetic to these people, she offers an alternative to their pushy, demanding form of witness. She presents this option in her description of the palo santo trees she saw growing on the shores of the Galapagos. She sees all people, she explains, as palo santo trees, "holy sticks, together watching all that we watch, and growing in silence" (*TST*, 74). She would like "to come back" as a palo santo tree, she decided on her second visit to the islands, "so that I could be, myself, a perfect witness, and look, mute, and wave my arms" (*TST*, 75). In Dillard's mind true witness can only be silent, as God himself is silent.

Chapter Six
Holding up the Universe

In 1982, along with her publication of *Teaching a Stone to Talk*, Dillard broke new ground in her career with her first book on the literary theory of contemporary fiction, *Living by Fiction*. Some critics, apparently rejecting her argument that fiction belongs to the people, declared her out of her league. They found *Living by Fiction* "amateurish" and full of "platitudes and vagueness . . . superficiality . . . dubious generalizations, half-truths and outright contradiction."[1] The majority of reviewers, however, responded favorably, even enthusiastically, and easily forgave Dillard for taking occasional shortcuts in logic or explication. As one commented, "So what; she's gutsy."[2] These admirers praised *Living by Fiction* as "stimulating," "challenging," "bold, provocative," and "maddening but enchanting."[3] "This is a book full of wonders," intoned one reviewer. "She is never dogmatic, always open-minded."[4]

In her introduction Dillard announces the primary subject of *Living by Fiction*: "This is, ultimately, a book about the world. It inquires about the world's meaning. It attempts to do unlicensed metaphysics in a teacup. The teacup at hand, in this case, is contemporary fiction."[5] In other words, her discussion of contemporary fiction is merely a springboard for approaching the broader subject of the meaning of the world. Dillard's working title for the book—"Fiction and the World's Meaning"[6]—perhaps stated this intent more unequivocally. A reader of *Living by Fiction* would do well to bear this purpose in mind. Mistaking Dillard's sole purpose as the discussion of contemporary fiction could easily lead to a complaint such as that voiced by one critic that "the subject she is writing about simply evaporates as the book progresses."[7] On the contrary, by the end of the book Dillard has narrowed in on her true subject, the meaning of the world—an issue that in one way or another she has addressed in all her previous books.

This is not to say that the discussion of contemporary fiction in *Living by Fiction* has no function. Dillard uses her discussion of fiction as a tool for examining the concept of meaning and for bridging the gap between the mind of the individual and the world at large. Generally, Dillard takes the constructionist view, which holds that the apparent meaning seen in the world is placed there by and takes the shape of the observing mind. As Dillard expresses it, "The mind fits the world and shapes it as a river fits and shapes its own banks" (*LBF*, 15). Fiction is an especially appropriate arena for examining this process of the construction of meaning, Dillard explains, because the basic function of fiction, and the one for which it is most perfectly suited, is to express a writer's thoughts about the world. Nor can it escape accomplishing this function as long as it uses words, for words are inextricably tied, as is the mind, to the world of things. From this point it is but a short leap—though certainly still a leap—to what one critic described as Dillard's "bold and surprising analogy between the world of texts and the world itself."[8]

Some of the enthusiasm that greeted *Living by Fiction* was an obvious reaction against the increasingly arcane nature of literary theory. In this context Dillard's clarity was a breath of fresh air. Critics declared *Living by Fiction* to be at the very least a useful introduction to the difficult subject of contemporary fiction. Reviewers seemed pleased and surprised at how much light it shed on its subject. As one explained, it "brings a remarkable degree of clarity to a much-muddled subject."[9] One reviewer found this achievement of clarity a "remarkable feat."[10] Another stated that *Living by Fiction* was "one of those rare books that makes thinking about criticism an act of lucid meditation."[11] Dillard accomplishes this clarity through a great sensitivity to both her subject and her readers, and through what one called a "charming concreteness" whenever the book's discussion grows difficult.[12]

In *Living by Fiction* Dillard's prose style, as usual, also attracted attention. Her informal, conversational tone disturbed some, one reviewer complaining about what he called her "unbuttoned prose" (Breslin, 4). Others praised her style as "lively, relaxed, and conversational."[13] The book "proceeds like wonderful conversation," praised another (Bourjaily, 22). Dillard's informal style, however, does not hide the care with which she has structured her prose. One reviewer exclaimed that her sentences "are shaped as carefully and fitted together as exactly as tiles in a Byzantine mosaic" (Moramarco, 8). Others hailed her prose as "sparkl[ing] like fireworks behind a hedge."[14] Several reviewers found that their reading of *Living by Fiction* was more than a mere passive intellectual exercise; rather, it became an experience that actively engaged their minds, "as enticing as fine conversation over a rich meal" (Price, 102). This stylistic excellence is the result of Dillard's decision, expressed in her introduction, to fling aside the "sensible approach" of a careful textual critic "in favor of enthusiasm, free speculation, blind assertion, dumb joking, and diatribe" (*LBF*, 14–15). It is her exuberance, her undaunted love of fiction, and her own search for understanding that carry the show.

Part 1: Some Contemporary Fiction

Chapter 1 of part 1, entitled "Fiction in Bits," introduces readers to what Dillard calls the contemporary modernist writers; their work is sometimes labeled, she explains, "fabulation," "experimental," "neo-Modernist," and "Post-Modernist." Some of the individuals she classifies in this broad group include Jorge Luis Borges, John Barth, Samuel Beckett, Vladimir Nabokov, Thomas Pynchon, Italo Calvino, Julio Cortázar, and Carlos Fuentes. Dillard does not believe a hard dividing line exists between these contemporary modernists and what she calls the historical modernists, such as Kafka, Joyce, Faulkner, and Woolf. The contemporaries, she maintains, are simply taking and extending the emphasis on surface that the historical modernists introduced.

Before going on to the contemporary modernists, Dillard discusses the methods introduced by the modernists and some of the philosophy behind their use. The trait Dillard cites as most typical of modernist fiction is its "shattering of narrative line" (*LBF*, 20), an effect accomplished through several means. First, time is smashed into tiny, unordered, rapidly shifting fragments, thereby turning the work into a kind of narrative collage that destroys the appearance of cause-and-effect relationship. This shattering of narration is increased, second, by rapid and extreme shifts in setting and, third, by rapid shifts in point of view. This presentation of events through the eyes of many different characters challenges the existence of an actual truth of the event; one viewpoint appears as likely as any other, thus promoting an attitude of extreme relativism. Dillard compares the worldview created by such techniques to the realities of quantum physics, whereby apparently meaningless events occur unhinged from cause and effect. Nothing is fixed or certain; all is undefined possibility.

In the middle of this discussion of modernist techniques in part 1 Dillard interrupts herself to make some important points about standards of artistic integrity. Modernist fiction often presents the view that life in today's society is a meaningless, disordered, relativistic, and disconnected experience. The portrayal of this experience in fiction may thus take a form that in previous ages would have been considered poor writing. In such a context discerning good from bad writing becomes a serious dilemma. Dillard presents this question in several ways: "When is a work 'about' meaninglessness and when is it simply meaningless?" (*LBF*, 25) or, to phrase it a little differently,

"If the writer's honest intention is to recreate a world he finds meaningless, must his work then be meaningless?" (*LBF,* 27). Dillard responds that it is artistic integrity that determines good writing, and that artistic integrity in turn depends on internal coherence.

For example, if portrayed through a system of intentionally structured unity, meaninglessness that is projected on the world by a work can paradoxically become the meaning of the work. Thus, it is the imposition of order on chaos, Dillard maintains, that creates art: "Art may imitate anything but disorder" (*LBF,* 28). The calculated and unified imposition of disorder on a text becomes a type of order. Arbitrariness, Dillard concludes, "must always be damning" (*LBF,* 29). Thus, she takes the classicist view that "the formal relationship among parts is the essential value of all works of art" (*LBF,* 34).

This digression about artistic integrity is followed by chapter 2, humorously but accurately titled "Two Wild Animals, Seven Crazies, and a Breast." Here Dillard shows how contemporary modernist fiction writers extend modernist techniques in the treatment of character, point of view, and narration. In contemporary modernist fiction, she explains, the main characters are no longer troubled individuals struggling to come to terms with the human condition. Rather, they are, as Dillard sums them up, "alien grotesques," barely recognizable as human beings, and sometimes not even human beings. She lists for example, 10 first-person narrators in recent fiction, including a cow, a paranoid schizophrenic, a dinosaur, and, of all things, a human breast.[15] Contemporary modernist writers, Dillard explains, flatten their characters and distance them, relegating them to a solely formal and structural role. Rather than representing members or even outcasts of a society, these characters become "focal points for action or idea" (*LBF,* 39). The extreme of this technique, Dillard observes, is that fiction of some contemporary modernists which contains no characters at all.

Dillard next explains the way in which contemporary modernist writers extended the use of point-of-view techniques developed by the historical modernists. The former took the narrator of the latter and used its limited consciousness to "erect a veil between us and things and between us and the forgetfulness which is total immersion" (*LBF,* 41). The effect, rather than a greater sense of intimacy, is a distancing of the reader from the action of the fiction. The use of multiple narrators magnifies this effect even further. Just as the use of grotesque or nonhuman characters makes the character merely a focal point for an idea, so the use of multiple narrators makes each event a focal point of artistic structure. Consciousness, self-consciousness, and imagination thus take the place of action and character.

The intrusion of the author into the work is another technique used by contemporary modernist writers to emphasize the surface art of their work. This interrupting presence prevents the reader from suspending disbelief and acts as a consistent reminder that the book is the work of a writer's imagination. The focus is no longer on the telling of a story. Narration becomes not only unnecessary but perhaps even a detriment to the work, a sign that it is in some way unartistic. As an example of this development, Dillard cites a reviewer who criticized the ending of a novel as being "plotty," as though that in itself were a condemnation of the work. She describes the movement of fiction in the twentieth century in terms of the following trends: "from depth to surface, from rondure to planes, from world to scheme, from observation to imagination, from story to theory, from society to individual, from emotion to mind" (*LBF,* 47). The work of art, she concludes, has become "a self-lighted opacity, not a window and not a mirror" (*LBF,* 47). The reader, then, must not enter the work of fiction but, rather, stay on its surface, since that is where the writer has spread its art.

In the last chapter of part 1, titled "The Fiction of Possibility," Dillard comments on the themes of contemporary modernist fiction. The emphasis in this century on self-consciousness, she surmises, is reflected in the common themes of contemporary modernist fiction: the nature of art, the nature of perception, and the nature of knowledge. Drawing connections between art and science, she briefly mentions some of the pioneers in the area of thought and perception—Bateson, Jakobson, Noam Chomsky, Lévi-Strauss, and others—who seek to understand "the processes by which the mind imposes order" (*LBF,* 54). She even anticipates the development of cognitive psychology as the new "hot topic" in this interdisciplinary coalition of science's great minds. They all seem to agree, she informs her reader, that "[t]he mind is itself an art object. It is a Mondrian canvas onto whose homemade grids it fits its preselected products. Our knowledge is contextual and only contextual" (*LBF,* 56).

Dillard concludes part 1 by describing contemporary modernist fiction as the "fiction of possibility." Fiction examines the process of knowing, which by necessity is the process of perception. But perception is achieved only through invention, imagination, and creation. We cannot know the world; we can only study our perception of the world. Each new piece of scientific "knowledge" invariably takes the form of the mind that anticipated it; discovery and imagination are indistinguishable. Likewise, in the world of art the mind of the artist determines the form the work will take: "If inventing is knowing, and if meaning is contextual, then the artist is the supreme knower and the artificer of meaning" (*LBF,* 60).

Rather than falling into the despair of relativism at this realization, Dillard views it as granting a new degree of importance to art. Art is the creation of contexts and thus the creation of everything, she maintains. She even promotes the artist to the role of God's assistant. The act of creating did not end at Genesis: it is "instead God's spendthrift and neverending jubilee" (*LBF*, 61). Here again we see the thread that runs through virtually all Dillard's works—the concept that the artist's work partakes of the divine.

In part 1 of *Living by Fiction* Dillard examines what might be called the leading edge of contemporary fiction. She deals with some of the more remarkable extremes to which contemporary modernist writers are pushing the techniques developed by their predecessors. Toward the end of part 1, however, she reminds her reader that most contemporary fiction writers are writing largely traditional fiction. While these writers make use of many of the modernists' techniques, they employ them in the service of traditional ends, producing "novels and stories of depth and power, novels and stories which penetrate the world and order it, which engage us intellectually and move us emotionally, which render complex characters in depth, treat moral concerns and issues" (*LBF*, 65). This is the mainstream of contemporary fiction, Dillard concludes in part 1.

Part 2: The State of the Art

In part 2 of *Living by Fiction* Dillard explains the forces in play that keep the mainstream of contemporary fiction within the realm of the traditional. In a chapter entitled "Revolution, No" she begins by discussing how language forms our perceptions and therefore also our knowledge of the world. Again emphasizing the unknowability of the world in any absolute sense, she describes language as "a fabricated grid someone stuck in a river." All perceptions and knowledge are shaped by language and determined by it: "I cannot tell you, because I do not know, what my language prevents my knowing" (*LBF*, 70). Although a writer cannot use language to signify things as they actually are, he can use language to do "an airtight job of signifying his *perceptions* of things as they are" (*LBF*, 70). This important distinction avoids problems of solipsism and takes into consideration current thought about the relationship between language and perception. Dillard wisely acknowledges that language does not need to know the world perfectly in order to accurately convey perceptions of the world.

The importance of Dillard's assertion—that is, that language can accurately communicate perceptions of the world—is that it allows her also to assert that the subject matter of fiction is necessarily tied to the world. The sole purpose and function of words, she appears to maintain, is the expression of perceptions about the world. She admits words can be so purified of meaning that they no longer reflect perceptions and become arbitrary sounds. Such was almost the case, Dillard suggests, in the work of Gertrude Stein and in Joyce's *Finnegans Wake*. But such a purified language would no longer be fiction and would no longer interest fiction readers. No such revolution will take place, Dillard maintains, because "fiction's materials are bits of the world" (*LBF*, 72). This fact limits the extremes to which fiction can go.

In her next chapter, "Marketplace and Bazaar," Dillard shows that another force keeping contemporary fiction from going off the deep end is the commercial market for fiction. More than any other art or literary genre, fiction is read by a broad spectrum of people with greatly varying interests and tastes. The majority of the members of this audience are not literary specialists in any sense of the word, and many have had little or no formal study of literature. This fact tends to keep fiction traditional, Dillard asserts, because nonspecialists tend to prefer depth over abstract surface. The size and breadth of the audience keep fiction loose and varied in both structure and subject matter. Unfortunately, Dillard admits, those audience traits also tend to encourage a certain degree of literary mediocrity.

While Dillard seems to believe that it is basically good for fiction to be responsive to the interests and preferences of nonspecialists, she seems uncomfortable with what she sees as a blurring between genres and even between literature and nonliterature. Despite this concern, she is open-minded enough to realize the difficulties in making such determinations. In fact, she spends several pages debating such distinctions as those between canon and literature, between the literary and the popular, between journalism and memoir, and between fiction and nonfiction. She provides no firm answers, only acknowledgment of the difficulties inherent in such categorizations. She concludes that the democratic nature of the fiction market, as well as the profit-making orientation of publishers, keeps it traditional. She also leaves the reader with the unsettling knowledge that these forces do not ensure that all the best work reaches the bookstores' shelves.

In "Who Listens to Critics?" Dillard suggests that criticism keeps fiction traditional in some ways but encourages contemporary modernism in other ways. She begins by saying that criticism does indeed have a great influence on the writing of fiction. This is true in the United States despite anti-intellectual and cult-of-personality tendencies that encourage the notion of the writer as a gifted, uneducated savage. Criticism influences writers,

Dillard says, because almost all contemporary fiction writers have been to college and in their studies have been exposed to careful textual analysis of one critical type or another.

Criticism keeps fiction traditional because college curricula focus on the English and American canon. English majors are often not exposed to European or Latin American fiction, which is much more modernist than British and American fiction. Students also usually learn tools of literary criticism that for the most part are applicable to every genre of literature and every historical period. This academic orientation, along with a de-emphasis on chronology, suggests to the student that new is not necessarily better, and that good literature can be found in every age. Dillard contrasts this attitude to the approach of art education, which stresses the revolutionary nature of modern and contemporary art. As she expresses it, "Young painters must look forward; young writers may look around" (*LBF*, 97).

In other ways literary criticism encourages contemporary modernism, perhaps largely because, Dillard says, any formalist textual analysis emphasizes values that are contemporary modernist in character. Limitation to the text stresses self-reference, for example, and analysis of structure stresses ingenuity and pattern. In addition, contemporary fiction writers are particularly responsive to criticism, sometimes parodying the critical essay itself. Dillard even suggests that contemporary modernist fiction resulted from the awareness of criticism, particularly awareness of the critical ideals of the Russian formalists and the New Critics. Dillard concludes her chapter by declaring the influence of criticism as predominantly contemporary modernist, rather than traditional. Contemporary fiction has "purified itself," she maintains, "through the agent of criticism" (*LBF*, 100).

Dillard concludes part 2 of *Living by Fiction* with a chapter about prose styles, "Fine Writing, Cranks, and the New Morality: Prose Styles." Here she discusses two strains of prose, labeling them the plain and the fancy. She begins with fancy, or fine, prose, which she thinks possesses complexity and grandeur. It is clear in this discussion that fine writing possesses Dillard's heart, even if plain writing possesses her mind. Her description of fine writing is, self-referentially, itself fine writing. It possesses the metaphors, bald similes, allusions, repetition, assonance, alliteration, and other traits she cites as typical of fine writing:

[Fine writing] is an energy. . . . It can penetrate very deep, piling object upon object to build a tower from which to breach the sky; it can enter with courage or bravura those fearsome realms where the end products of art meet the end products of thought, and where perfect clarity is not possible. Fine writing is not a mirror, not a window, not a document, not a surgical tool. It is an artifact and an achievement; it is at once an exploratory craft and the planet it attains; it is a testimony to the possibility of the beauty and penetration of written language. (*LBF*, 106)

Dillard discusses the various uses to which fine writing can be put, to further both modernist and contemporary modernist aims. She concludes her discussion by commenting that fine writing is always subject to the accusation that it sacrifices accuracy for the "dubious value" of beauty (*LBF*, 116). She objectively presents the arguments against fine writing, but her heart doesn't seem to be in her comments about its criticism. Fine writing—or "overwriting," as Dillard's critics often call it—seems to be in her blood.

On the side of plain prose, which Dillard calls "a kind of literary vernacular," are clarity, strength, accuracy, and a spare kind of beauty (*LBF*, 119). She explains that while it is often used to distance, it can also be used to express tenderness and respect. Plain prose is necessary, she maintains, for handling violent or emotional scenes without evoking extreme emotionalism in the reader. It also suggests a modesty and an objectivity on the part of the writer by respectfully allowing readers to form their own thoughts and feelings rather than being told what to think and feel. Dillard ends her discussion of prose styles by comparing them to the training of a puppy to look where its master points, instead of looking at the master's hand. With fine prose, Dillard explains, the writer tells the reader, "Look at my hand." With plain prose, he says instead, "Look over there." The best fiction, she concludes, does both.

Part 3: Does the World Have Meaning?

In part 3 Dillard finally gets to the real topic of the book: the nature of meaning. She begins with a chapter entitled "The Hope of the Race," a reference to the seemingly universal human desire for meaning. Consistent with her view of the artist as performing a religious function, she sees criticism as "a kind of modern focusing of the religious impulse, the hope of the race: the faith that something has meaning" (*LBF*, 127).

She examines three critical positions about the existence and discoverability of meaning in art. The first, which she calls "quasi-structuralist," asserts that both art and criticism fail to refer meaningfully to anything because of the self-referential and arbitrary nature of language. Critics holding this position, Dillard says, stress the playful, artificial, and irresponsible nature of all mental effort. The second, less extreme position toward meaning in art is that the art object is itself unknowable. Here Dillard quotes

Harold Bloom for the assertion that all interpretations are misinterpretations and therefore are themselves only prose poetry. The third position, and the one to which Dillard subscribes, is that interpretation of texts is possible because they "use a shared language which refers, however clumsily, to a shared world" (*LBF,* 130). While we may never completely exhaust the meaning of a text, that does not imply nothing can be known about its meaning. Dillard points out that interpretation is not an exact science and cannot fairly be restricted only to those things that are definite. She understands enough about science to conclude that it too is not so certain. In fact, all knowledge is based on interpretation, Dillard argues, and all branches of knowledge are merely prose poetry to those who embrace "[p]rofound epistemological skepticism and the blithe relativism which accompanies it" (*LBF,* 132).

Meaning is indeed possible, Dillard concludes in this chapter, and establishing it is part of the human endeavor. The criterion for meaning, however, is not truth but rather consensus—the same standard that governs all interpretive conclusions, even those within the arena of the so-called hard sciences. Further, meaning, which is a human concept, exists only in relation to human activities. This distinction in fact determines who is sane and who is schizophrenic, Dillard correctly reminds her reader. Human activities and artifacts are subject to interpretation; natural objects and events are not. Dillard's commonsense approach is impressively simple and difficult to refute. As she sums it up, "All interpreters are like critics in this way: they require that someone else has been there first" (*LBF,* 141).

At the end of the chapter "The Hope of the Race" Dillard posits the central question of the book, whether the methods of literary criticism can be used to interpret the world. She responds that we can certainly do so if we believe that the world is a text that has been purposefully fashioned by some great author in the sky. Unfortunately, no one has been willing to do that since the American transcendentalists, and before them the medieval European philosophers. Apparently abandoning the idea of direct interpretation of the world, Dillard takes another tack, and that is to turn to fiction.

Chapter 9 is entitled "Can Fiction Interpret the World?" If we aren't willing to say that some supernatural entity has "written" the world, thereby making it subject to interpretation, we can still indirectly approach the issue of meaning in the world by looking through the eyes of the fiction writer. Like that of the theologian, the work of the fiction writer, Dillard states, is a human artifact and is therefore subject to interpretation. It is also by her definition able to contain meaning that can be reasonably, if not certainly or absolutely, determined through criticism, or interpretation. The standard for determining good interpretation is, we remember, consensus, not truth.

But Dillard does not stop here; she goes one step further by arguing that the fiction writer is in a sense actually interpreting the world, or at least interpreting his own experience of the world. This implication represents a return to the issue she earlier appeared to abandon, that is, whether the world can be directly interpreted. She is quick to admit that fiction, because of the creative component involved, is not purely or strictly interpretation. The fiction writer's purpose is partly to interpret his experience of the world, but he does so by creating an alternate world that becomes the arena for his observations and impressions. That alternate world comprises bits and pieces of the world itself. Because the world is the source of materials from which the fiction writer builds the alternate world, he is concerned with the world, studies it closely, and seeks to "render as much of the world as he possibly can as coherent as he possibly can." Thus, Dillard concludes, the writer "approaches the world exactly as a critic approaches a text" (*LBF,* 151): with the aim of rendering it as coherent as possible.

With this step Dillard has created an analogy between the world and a text, an analogy that allows her, in the book's final chapter, Chapter 11, to reinsert meaning into the world from which skepticism had previously drained meaning. Before moving to that point, however, she has several other points to make. At the end of chapter 9 she discusses quality in fiction, based on her view that part of the function of fiction is to interpret the world. Because most thinking people recognize complexity, subtlety, and breadth in their experience of the world, these same traits should be reflected in good fiction, Dillard argues. Superficial or simplistic treatments in fiction do not represent excellence, for the experience of the world is neither superficial nor simplistic. The best fiction writers, Dillard seems to suggest, are those whose techniques—whether traditional, modernist, or contemporary modernist—interest the thinking reader in inquiring more deeply into an understanding of the writer's experience of the world as presented in the work.

In Chapter 10, "About Symbol, and with a Diatribe against Purity," Dillard discusses the function of symbol as a cognitive tool. Here again she draws connections between art and religion: "Any work of art symbolizes the process by which spirit generates matter, or materials generate idea. Any work of art symbolizes the juncture itself, the socketing of eternity into time and energy into form" (*LBF,* 164). Dillard goes further, suggesting that the nature of symbolism reflects the nature of knowledge in the sense that both are approximate and not subject to precise or empirical summary. She views symbol as a cognitive tool that opens up "new and hitherto inaccessible regions," and, remarkably, she maintains that "there is no boundary, and probably no difference, between symbol and the realm it comes to mean" (*LBF,* 167). She takes as an example the story of Christ: "An art object, say, and a myth are each the agent and the object of cognition. Each is a lens focused on itself. Say that the story of Christ is a symbol. Say that generations of thinkers have enlarged and enriched the symbol. What then? What is the difference between this narrative, or this artifact, and what it symbolizes? It is it, itself" (*LBF,* 167).

Dillard states that all knowledge is, generally speaking, symbolic and that delving deeply into any body of knowledge requires faith in its symbols. From this Dillard presents the parenthetical but fascinating principle that "faith is the requisite of knowledge" (*LBF,* 168). Symbols act, she explains, at the level "where the scarcely understood fades into the unknown," and as a result, symbols are somewhat "unmanageable," something like "an enthusiastic and ill-trained Labrador retriever which yanks you into traffic" (*LBF,* 168–69). She concludes that both symbols and art objects manifest things "in their fullness," rather than standing for things: "You begin by using symbols, and end by contemplating them" (*LBF,* 170).

The last chapter of *Living by Fiction* has the same title as part 3: "Does the World Have Meaning?" Dillard begins the chapter with the whimsical idea that by creating order the work of art helps counteract the force of entropy in the universe. If this is the case, as she would clearly like to think it is, then "[a] completed novel in a trunk in the attic is an order added to the sum of the universe's order" (*LBF,* 174). Dillard calls this position the "most extreme, cheerful, and fantastic view of art" to which she ever subscribes (*LBF,* 173).

In the book's last pages she returns to the question of whether artists discover order or invent it, even though she says it is "some mule-headedness" that compels us to continue to ask this question. She concludes, as she did in chapter 3 of part 1, that invention and discovery are the same process: "It is all fiction" (*LBF,* 179). Still, here she seems uncomfortable with the conclusion, particularly with the idea that all order is merely a projection of some inner structure of the brain. She calls the latter notion "the most dismal view—of art and of everything—I can imagine" (*LBF,* 182). She would prefer to believe that order is not just "a perceptual trick" of the mind but, rather, "actual": "Either we bring it forth by creating it . . . or we discern it with our minds and senses and art, generation by generation, discovering bits of the puzzle now here, now there" (*LBF,* 184).

In the end Dillard refuses to give hard-and-fast answers to the many questions she has posed for herself and her readers. She ends the book with a final comment about whether meaning is in the world or in our minds: "I am sorry; I do not know" (*LBF*, 185). While some critics saw this conclusion as dodging the issue, it is the one line in the book that is most characteristic of Dillard. Never one to take the easy way out, she won't let her readers do so either. In one sense this apparently flippant comment is especially appropriate and even self-referential, for it illustrates the quality of intellectual integrity that Dillard identifies as the cornerstone of good art.

Chapter Seven

Testing Spirits with a Plumb Line

Encounters with Chinese Writers was published in 1984. The first half of the book describes Dillard's experiences in May and June 1982 as a member of a six-person delegation of U.S. scholars, writers, and publishers traveling in China. As she explains in her introduction, the delegation spent 10 days in Beijing meeting with writers and then traveled to Xian, Hangzhou, Nanjing, and Shanghai. The second half of the book describes her experiences in September of that year, when she helped host a U.S.–Chinese Writers Conference in Los Angeles and accompanied the Chinese visitors on part of their tour of the United States, including visits to Disneyland, Dillard's own Wesleyan University, Harvard, and Walden Pond. Dillard explains that during her trip to China she met two of the writers who later came to the writers' conference.

Weighing in at only 105 pages, *Encounters with Chinese Writers* is a deceptively small book. In characteristic understatement Dillard says it contains "mostly anecdotes—moments—from which few generalizations may be drawn except perhaps about Chinese—and human—complexity."[1] Its brief, anecdotal nature nonetheless struck some as superficial. One reviewer declared, for instance, that Dillard does not get beyond "the stereotypical cardboard figures of 'official' China."[2] Another flippantly labeled *Encounter with Chinese Writers* "just confetti" and declaimed its "hit or miss quality."[3]

In her introduction Dillard states that her interest was not in getting "to the bottom of 'the truth about China'" (*ECW*, 4). In fact, she expressed doubt that such "truth" could be achieved. To her statement that the book contains mostly anecdotes she has appended an inconspicuous and off-handed statement of her true intent: to illustrate the rich complexity of the human spirit. This is far-reaching, and the wonder is that Dillard has successfully put so much into such a small package. In this regard the nature of her book parallels human nature itself. The personality of a given individual may appear misleadingly narrow, but a closer look reveals a profound depth that may in fact be bottomless. It is this profound depth that Dillard has chosen to illuminate in *Encounters with Chinese Writers* by describing carefully selected and painstakingly drawn incidents. Critics who noticed Dillard's methods delighted in her "montage of wit and insight" and her "easy charm."[4] As one admirer perceptively recognized, it is "no less largeminded or surprising in its observations" than *Pilgrim at Tinker Creek* or *Teaching a Stone to Talk*.[5] *Encounters with Chinese Writers* shows that Dillard is still concerned with mystery, this time the mystery of the human mind. She explains the purpose of the book's anecdotes as follows: "Their subject is not China per se; their subject is the paradoxical nature of all of our days, the curious way we bump up against the unexpected everywhere, the endless dramas of good will in bad times, the sheer comedy of human differences and cultural differences, and the courage and even whimsy with which we—all of us—cope" (*ECW*, 3–4).

Dillard uses many techniques to underscore her point that human complexity— Chinese, American, or any other—is paradoxical and beyond the grasp of the rational mind. Throughout the book she uses the verb *fathom*, with its connotations of almost-immeasurable depth, in connection with individuals' attempts to understand one another. The Chinese, for example, cannot "fathom" the "essentially democratic instincts" of an American Hollywood writer who is their host one evening (*ECW*, 67). Dillard shows that this distance between individuals also occurs between individuals of the same culture. In a translated quotation from one of the Chinese writers' books, a fictitious wife admits she cannot "fathom" her husband's silence (*ECW*, 72). Dillard's first chapter, "A Man of the World," is practically an allegory of this theme. In it Dillard tells of sensing that in the intent gaze of a dignified Chinese gentlemen, whom she calls Wu Fusan, he is "testing my spirit with a plumb line" and "sizing up my spirit, my heart and strength, my capacity for commitment" (*ECW*, 13–14). This incident is reminiscent of Dillard's story of locking eyes with the weasel in "Living Like Weasels"; in both instances the participants are each examining, measuring, sizing up their opponents.

Dillard's first reaction to Wu Fusan illustrates the importance of looking carefully—another common theme of Dillard's, here applied to human interaction rather than nature. Her impression of the gentleman, even after watching him for several days, is that he is "a hack, a politico, a man of the world without depth of interest." "I am, as usual, wrong," she abruptly concludes this description (*ECW*, 12). Her locking of gazes with the man convinces her that he possesses a remarkable sophistication, even a wisdom, about human nature. It is an important lesson for her, one she applies profitably during the ensuing interactions with the Chinese. She intently observes every nuance of word and action, struggling to "plumb their depths," just as hers had been plumbed.

In the incident just described, and throughout *Encounters with Chinese Writers*, Dillard emphasizes the extreme subtlety and sophistication of the Chinese. Theirs is an ancient culture, one that has been worn smooth and polished by thousands of years of history. When Dillard asks an Italian friend about the gaze of Wu Fusan, she tells Dillard that the ability to size up another individual is the particular area of expertise of the Chinese. Her friend explains that Chinese literature is about only one thing, "the human spirit in all its depth and complexity." As a result of this skill, she continues, "There is nothing they do not already understand. It makes them peaceful, at ease with all people" (*ECW*, 15).

In contrast to this sophistication of the Chinese, the Americans Dillard describes in *Encounters with Chinese Writers* appear childlike and innocent, even stupid. The Chinese, while polite and respectful to an extreme, clearly do not often think highly of their guests. In fact, Dillard tells her readers, one of the Americans' Chinese guides is a professional host of foreign delegations; his fellow Chinese refer to him as a *waiban*, which translates to "barbarian handler" (*ECW*, 17). Indeed, Dillard senses that sometimes the Chinese are wary of the Americans, fearing perhaps that they might start jumping on the furniture or breaking windows. She observes that, for some of her Chinese hosts, interacting with the Americans is like "talking to young children about what you did in the war": plainly the children in their ignorance will never stumble on the subjects that to the speaker are so painful (*ECW*, 17–18).

Dillard suspects, however, that the childlike quality of the Americans is in some ways endearing to the Chinese, as it in fact sometimes is to Dillard herself. This idea is humorously and poignantly illustrated during the writers' conference, which was held in a UCLA auditorium. One of the Chinese writers, a woman named Zhang Jie, suddenly dragged Dillard across the auditorium to show her a huge security guard with a large weapon at the door of the auditorium. Rather than being frightened, Zhang Jie was fascinated by the tall, handsome young man, and wanted to have her picture taken with him. After the incident, Dillard chatted with the guard, who was, in Dillard's words, "big and bashful." He was embarrassed by his weapons and begged Dillard to assure the Chinese that he was there to protect them: "I'm their friend." The encounter with this fellow American touched Dillard, and she exclaimed, "And I am smitten with one of those rushes of feeling for this country which overtakes me often when I am with the Chinese" (*ECW*, 71).

Despite the great sophistication of the Chinese, Dillard skillfully shows that, paradoxically, they also possess a great ordinariness. Human nature is the same the world around, Dillard suggests. When accompanying the Chinese writers on their travels in the United States, Dillard notes with satisfaction that they act just as the Americans did in China—almost uncontrollably excited. In the relaxed and fun-filled context of sight-seeing, she enjoys the Chinese, as they cavort at Disneyland, balance spoons on their noses with Dillard in a Boston restaurant, collect one souvenir after another, and pose for photographs. By the end of Dillard's travels with the group, the Chinese and their American hosts are one big happy family, even singing old American favorites together on the bus ride back to the campus.

But paradox is always at the heart of human nature, Dillard reminds her readers throughout *Encounters with Chinese Writers*. No matter how well she gets to know her Chinese friends, they still continue to surprise her. One particularly bashful, nervously giggling Chinese woman, for instance, turns out to be the most controversial and antiestablishment of the writers she met in Beijing. In another instance a young Chinese interpreter shocks Dillard with his knowledge of medieval Western art. And one night after dinner one Chinese writer after another bursts into melodious song.

Dillard gives much attention in *Encounters with Chinese Writers* to Zhang Jie, who appears to be her personal favorite among the Chinese visitors. She is a fascinating mass of contradictions. While she is sophisticated and elegant, she is also capable of being playful and lighthearted. She is a pragmatic, hardheaded Communist but also an extreme idealist. She is confident and determined, yet often collapses into giggles. Dillard struggles to capture her essence in a series of descriptions: "Zhang Jie . . . touches people warmly, cocks her wide head in a rush of sentiment; her eyes flash with sarcasm; she weeps, points an accusing finger, toes the line, springs around on her long legs in their low heels" (*ECW*, 65).

Despite all this lightheartedness in *Encounters with Chinese Writers*, Dillard also shows the dark side of being a Chinese writer. She describes, for instance, the persecution of intellectuals that occurred during the 10-year Cultural Revolution from 1966 until 1976. During that period, by the Chinese's own figures 100 million people were persecuted, with up to 850,000 deaths by beating or suicide. Most of the writers and intellectuals Dillard met had suffered to one degree or another; one couple had been in solitary confinement, in separate jails, for three years. In 1976 the Chinese government began working to "rehabilitate" 500,000 intellectuals back into society. Yet although writers were freer than ever before in their lives, they were still subject to government control, and many topics continued to be off limits, including writing depicting the suffering that had occurred during the Cultural Revolution.

Throughout her interactions with the Chinese, Dillard is impressed with their willingness to sacrifice for their country. The sacrifice required of the writer is, we have seen, a frequent theme of Dillard's work. But the sacrifice of the American writer pales by comparison with that of these dedicated Chinese men and women. Nor does Dillard sense that the patriotism they express is forced, out of fear of future persecution; it is a genuine, absolute devotion to their nation and their culture. If *Encounters with Chinese Writers* contains any element of judgment against either culture, it is perhaps censure of the Americans for their lack of willingness to sacrifice for the good of their nation. Dillard recognizes that contemporary American writing can be viewed only as decadent and meaningless by the Chinese writers, whose only purpose in writing is to help their nation.

Dillard's tone indicates she is embarrassed by the self-involvement and selfishness of most Americans, including, in some respects, herself. "My life has set me at little risk, put me under no hardship," she admits (*ECW*, 14). She points out that Chinese writers live with the idea of sacrifice and with the knowledge of lives only recently lost. Their willingness to speak up and take any position at all appears remarkably courageous under the circumstances. She turns critically to her own countrymen, including herself in the criticism: "For what have we sacrificed? We well-fed writers are free to take potshots at our institutions from our couches" (*LBF*, 22).

In addition to the lack of cultural freedom in China, Dillard points out the material sacrifices with which its citizens must live. The extreme shortage of resources in the densely populated land makes every choice of land use a critical decision. Even the decision to publish books, for example, represents a sacrifice in a land where trees are scarce. Dillard explains that books are a great treasure in China and are usually available only to those whose jobs might require them. In such a context of scarcity every decision becomes crucial, requiring a degree of responsibility and care that is unimaginable for Americans. Dillard tells of one of her fellow writers who got lost in Shanghai. A young Chinese man who knew a little English generously offered to walk him back to the hotel, which turned out to be five or six miles away. For several miles of the trip the young man bragged about the bicycle he owned, apparently feeling rich by comparison to his fellow countrymen. But when he realized that this American had a car, he fell suddenly silent, saddened and embarrassed by his comparative poverty.

Dillard uses the difficulty of understanding another culture's literature as a metaphor for the difficulty of "plumbing the depths" of a culture different from one's own. She describes the difficulty the Chinese writers have under-standing the purpose behind contemporary Western experimental litera-ture. Without a deep understanding of the context—that is, the culture in which it developed—it must appear meaningless. Similarly, she reports hav-ing great difficulty herself seeing merit in even the best of Chinese literature, which seems simplistic to an American reader. Still, she realizes what an in-surmountable task it would be to gain an adequate knowledge of another culture's literary context. This point is forcefully brought home when the Chinese writers ask the Americans which American or English works they should translate first. The American writers are utterly speechless, knowing only too well how nonsensical their culture's greatest works will appear to even a knowledgeable Chinese reader. One American offers, humorously perhaps, *Lolita*, and is quickly kicked by one of his compatriots. It is a problem without an apparent solution.

Many of the incidents described in the foregoing discussion illustrate the humor with which Dillard presents these vignettes; however, not enough can be said to show how perfectly her humor suits her subject and furthers her purpose. Dillard is always at her best when telling a story, and in *En-counters with Chinese Writers* she gets the chance to tell one story after an-other. Her parents would be proud—her delivery is perfect. But here humor plays a role more critical than that of mere entertainment. It becomes a sine qua non of the human spirit, a symbol for the resilience that keeps human-kind going through all the difficulty and sorrow inherent in the human con-dition. It also helps further demonstrate the gap between the two cultures as the breakdown in communication between the two groups becomes in some cases downright hilarious. "Conversation has a pleasingly surreal quality," Dillard notes. She explains, for instance, the shock that always greets her when she attempts to say hello in Chinese. "I have no idea what I am actu-ally saying," she states helplessly (*ECW*, 78).

Despite the cultural chasm separating them, somehow the American and Chinese writers managed to reach each other, and that perhaps is the miracle of *Encounters with Chinese Writers*. Dillard tells the touching story of 74-year-old Chen Baichen, a short, dignified man who knows no English. He suffered the misfortune, Dillard is somewhat aghast to report, of being acci-dentally lost in Disneyland. When he was finally reunited with his group, she and some of the others momentarily forgot formalities and hugged him joyfully. She watched in surprise as his "enormous eyes" filled with tears, his emotions overcome by the warmth of their embraces (*ECW*, 83).

Encounters with Chinese Writers shows once again the startling breadth of Dillard's talents and establishes once and for all her ability to deal as effectively with human beings as with nature. Her clarity and simplicity emphasize the intangibility of the book's subject—the beautiful complexity of the human spirit. Perhaps the most remarkable accomplishment of the book is that it returns our gaze finally back to our own people and culture, with the added benefit of new insights. As one reviewer noted, in *Encounters with Chinese Writers* Dillard is able to "slash through much of our smugness about our social problems, our superiority, our literary pretensions" (Eis, 907). In the end the book is a mirror held up to human culture, forcing us to view ourselves from another angle and, perhaps, to reassess our former view of ourselves and others.

Conclusion

Prying out the Present, Tearing into the Future

This chapter poses the challenging task of summing up Dillard's career and anticipating its future directions. One thing is certain about her career so far: she has earned her reputation as an essayist, despite occasional excursions into other genres. Dillard explains her continuing interest in the essay in her introduction to *The Best American Essays—1988*, for which she served as guest editor. There she repeats the sentiment she has expressed off and on over the years: "The essay can do everything a poem can do, and everything a short story can do."[1] She seems more comfortable than ever before with that statement, perhaps because the essay has finally been accepted—although *reaccepted* is a more accurate term—as a literary form. The essay is superior to the short story, she asserts, because the essay is not limited by the need for "contrived entrances of long-winded characters" and "fabricated dramatic occasions" to set up its discussions of thoughts and ideas (*Best Essays*, xvi). In addition, the essay is superior to the poem in its capacity for metaphor, discursive idea, character, story, figurative language, and other poetic techniques. As Robert Atwan explains in his foreword to her edition, "Today's essayists are developing a prose that lives along the borders of fiction and poetry" (*Best Essays*, x).

In her introduction to *The Best American Essays—1988* Dillard briefly relates the history of the essay over the past 300 years. She reminds readers that in the eighteenth and nineteenth centuries essays were considered literary. Fiction, on the other hand, was for all practical purposes considered trash. By some great irony, the tables were turned in the twentieth century, with the essay getting the short end of the stick. Because of the attitude that nonfiction was not an art form, writers not infrequently disguised their nonfiction as fiction, merely to ensure that it got a "serious" reading. Long nonfiction works were passed off as novels, and essays were in many cases presented as short stories.

Dillard gives the scientist and writer Loren Eiseley the lion's share of the credit for reestablishing the place of the essay within "imaginative literature." He did so, she explains, by extending its symbolic capacity, making "meaningful symbols of both private and universal facts" (*Best Essays*, xv). She expresses her own special interest in this type of narrative essay that mixes plain facts and symbolic facts. Because of the growing recognition of its artistic capacity, Dillard concludes, "The essay has apparently . . . joined the modern world" (*Best Essays*, xx). She cites many other modern and contemporary nonfiction writers for their contribution to the development of the form—and modestly omits from this history the great part her own work has played in this regard.

Just how far the essay has come in the past decade can be seen by Dillard's prefatory comment to *Teaching a Stone to Talk*, in 1982. Because of the tentative position of the essay even then, she felt the need to point out and almost to apologize that her essays were "her real work, such as it is."[2] Now she is acknowledged as one of the foremost American essayists, and the label is no longer deprecatory. As she points out in her introduction to *The Best American Essays—1988*, writers need no longer disguise their non-fiction as fiction. Part of the purpose of the volume, she asserts, is to further encourage essay writers "out of the closet" (*Best Essays*, xiv).

In her introduction Dillard also points out some of the reasons the essay is especially appealing to her. First, she considers the essay peculiarly American, arguing that American literature "derives from the essay and hinges on the essay, if only because American literature springs from Emerson and Emerson was an essayist" (*Best Essays*, xvii). To further support this assertion, she cites the large quantity of nonfiction writing of prominent American writers, such as Melville, Hawthorne, Poe, and Twain. Second, the essay is well suited for dealing with history, one of Dillard's own favorite topics. In recent interviews she has expressed a growing interest in history, an interest demonstrated by her extensive treatment of the topic in *An American Childhood*. Third, the essay is especially able to treat the theme of knowing and what Dillard calls "unknowing, the unknowingness that is the nub of any intimacy." In a startling metaphor she describes the role of the essay in investigating knowability: "We try to see in the dark; we toss up our questions and they catch in the trees" (*Best Essays*, xxi).

If we agree with Dillard that American literature springs from Emerson and his essays, then we must conclude that Dillard herself is the paradigm of the contemporary American writer, for if ever a writer sprang from Emerson, and if ever a writer dedicated her career to the modernization of the Emersonian essay, it is Dillard who has done so. In Atwan's foreword to *The Best American Essays—1988* he describes some of the traits of what he calls the "new spirit of the American essay" (*Best Essays*, x). Although the volume contains none of Dillard's essays, his descriptions sound like a catalog of her own work. The new essay, he maintains, blurs criticism, biography, and exposition; it is autobiographical; and it often reads "just like a short story." In the war for the acceptance of the essay as a literary form, Dillard has been on the front lines since the beginning of her career.

The content of Dillard's work—as well as its structure—fits squarely within the American tradition. Undeniably, the greatest influence on her work is the American romantic and transcendentalist movements. But she has moved past those greats who were her teachers—Emerson, Melville, Thoreau, and others. She is in the fullest sense a contemporary writer because she voices the concerns of thinking men and women living in the late twentieth century. While the questions she confronts are often universal and timeless, each is colored by the special perspective of humanity in the late twentieth century.

Where will Dillard go from here? In a recent telephone conversation she described to me her current project: expanding her short story "The Living" into the novel she has been promising her readers for many years. She describes the novel as "dark, very dark," and expects it to take several more years to complete. Having already demonstrated her talents in the forms of the essay, poetry, literary criticism, and the memoir, Dillard's foray into the genre of fiction rounds out her repertoire. All her works, however, show her interest in the following three concerns, which are also certain to play a major role in her novel based on "The Living," as well as future works.

First, Dillard is concerned with the nature of human consciousness. In *Encounters with Chinese Writers* she showed how impossible it was to "plumb" the profound depths of the human mind. In *An American Childhood* she traced the development of consciousness through her own childhood. "What does it feel like to be alive?" she queried, and answered, "Living, you stand under a waterfall. You leave the sleeping shore deliberately; you shed your dusty clothes, pick your barefoot way over the high, slippery rocks, hold your breath, choose your footing, and step into the waterfall. The hard water pelts your skull, bangs in bits on your shoulders and arms. . . . It is time pounding at you, time."[3]

Part of human consciousness is what Dillard calls being "awake," that is, being aware, as much as possible, of all that goes on around us. Much of *An American Childhood* was her puzzling over how this awareness gradually comes into being. It is the growing recognition that a world and other people lie beyond our own limited existence. In her memoir Dillard describes this process variously as waking up or as surfacing. It does not happen all at once but, rather, comes and goes many times when we are children. Dillard describes this process during her own youth: "And still I break up through the skin of awareness a thousand times a day, as dolphins burst through seas, and dive again, and rise, and dive" (*AAC*, 210).

Part of being aware is realizing the part we play in human society. Dillard explains that as children we are aware only of our own needs and desires. But slowly our horizons expand and we become aware of our families, our friends, our neighbors, the state and nation we live in, and even the universe that contains it all. If we are lucky, we also become aware of our place within history and the fact that we are at the end of the long scarf of time unwinding. We are not isolated entities but are connected with all people and things. This fact bears a great responsibility: "You are accountable for everything. You are accountable for all that you do not know as well as all that you do; so you had better take notice, learn everything, and watch your sweet step."[4]

The second preoccupation throughout Dillard's work is the nature of suffering and death. In *Pilgrim at Tinker Creek* she confronted the horror of suffering and death in the animal kingdom; the nightmarish description of the frog being sucked dry by the giant water bug became her central image for the almost-unimaginable horror present in the world. In *Holy the Firm* she faced pain in the more human form of the child Julie Norwich, horribly burned and disfigured. Throughout her work, she has struggled with these realities of pain, trying desperately to reconcile them with her belief in a loving God. But Dillard's intense awareness of God's many gifts of grace do not allow her to reject her view of a loving God. As a result, she finds herself in a quandary, forced to admit that God allows suffering and death but also that his love for humankind is without bound. As she writes in "The Deer at Providencia," "These things are not issues; they are mysteries" (*TST*, 64).

Dillard also examines less tangible suffering—the emotional kind. In her essays and poems she portrays loneliness, heartbreak, loss, disappointment, and alienation. She speaks from firsthand experience when she concludes that we find pain not at the periphery of our lives but "at the center of human experience" ("Foreword," xiv). Dillard is no romantic. She knows that no amount of wishful thinking can transform the reality of human existence into a fairy-tale land where everyone lives happily ever after. This awareness of suffering, together with her determination to face it squarely and honestly, adds to her work an astonishing degree of emotional and intellectual integrity.

Dillard's third major concern is how we should live our lives in the face of the certainty of suffering and death. She suggests we must make our own rules as we go along; no one else can make them for us. She agrees with Emerson that life poses for each person "the same impossible task: forging an original relationship with the universe."⁵ *Forging* is the key word here, for we are indeed making something from nothing. In *The Writing Life* Dillard uses the process of writing as a metaphor for the process of living. Her title has a double meaning—it can mean the life of the writer or the life that *is being written.* The implication of the latter is that we write our lives as we go, creating whatever meaning we need to make them livable. Like the inchworm she describes in *The Writing Life*, we are stepping out onto thin air, but still we must somehow find a foothold.

What has Dillard "written" for her own life? What rules does she follow? One thread runs through all her writing—the certainty that we must throw ourselves into life. "Caring passionately about something isn't against nature, and it isn't against human nature. It's what we're here to do."⁶ In *An American Childhood* the child Dillard is impressed when an adult chases her for blocks after she and some friends hit his car with snowballs. When he does not give up until he catches her, she is amazed that "this ordinary adult evidently knew what I thought only children knew: that you have to fling yourself at what you're doing, you have to point yourself, forget yourself, aim, dive" (*AAC*, 39). This is the tenacity of "The Weasel," which bites and never lets go—not even to save its own life.

The certainty of death makes this attitude all the more critical. We must live each day taking into account the full knowledge that we will die. This is precisely the message of "The Living": the protagonist's life is transformed when a sadistic psychopath promises to kill him at some unspecified date in the future. The villain's aim is to gain power over his victim by putting him in continual fear. Paradoxically, the reverse occurs. As the villain watches his victim go about his life, he is puzzled and enraged to see a new sense of peace appear in his victim's face. In his perverted desire for power, he has unknowingly bestowed on his "victim" the greatest gift of all—the ability to live each moment to the fullest.

Living life to its fullest, generously, courageously, and honestly—this is the concern of Annie Dillard. It is the way of the artist. And so she throws herself into her work, sacrificing whatever she must, confronting whatever dangers she must, but giving all that she has, without a second thought. She explains, "One of the few things I know about writing is this: spend it all, shoot it, play it, lose it, all, right away, every time . . . give it, give it all, give it now."⁷ In *The Writing Life* Dillard describes a stunt pilot who, she felt, embodied this attitude. With every performance, he threw himself into his art, knowing that someday it would probably kill him. Dillard tells us that in fact it eventually did kill him. She writes:

Rahm used the plane inexhaustibly, like a brush marking thin air. His was pure energy and naked spirit. I have thought about it for years. Rahm's line unrolled in time. Like music, it split the bulging rim of the future along its seam. It pried out the present. We watchers waited for the split-second curve of beauty in the present to reveal itself. The human pilot, Dave Rahm, worked in the cockpit right at the plane's nose; his very body tore into the future for us and reeled it down upon us like a curling peel. . . . He brought the plane down on a far runway. After a pause, I saw him step out, an ordinary man, and make his way back to the terminal. (*WL*, 96–97).

Dillard also tears into the future with her art, and reels it down on us like a curling peel. When she steps back, like Rahm, she is an ordinary woman, heading for the terminal. Who can believe it?

Notes and References

Chapter One

1. John F. Baker, "Story behind the Book: *Pilgrim at Tinker Creek,*" *Publishers Weekly*, 18 March 1974, 28.
2. Dillard also stated as early as 1977 that she would like to write a novel. In fact, she is currently expanding "The Living" into a novel.
3. Michael Burnett, "An Interview with Annie Dillard," *Fairhaven Review* (1978): 90; hereafter cited in text.
4. Burnett, 90; Philip Yancey, "A Face Aflame: An Interview with Annie Dillard," *Christianity Today*, 5 May 1978, 960; hereafter cited in text.
5. Charles Trueheart, "Annie Dillard's Pilgrim's Progress," *Washington Post*, 28 October 1987, sec. D, 1; hereafter cited in text.
6. Annie Dillard, *Teaching a Stone to Talk: Expeditions and Encounters* (New York: Harper and Row, 1982), 30.
7. Robert Lindsey, "Annie Dillard, Far from Tinker Creek," *New York Times*, 9 November 1977, sec. C, 7; hereafter cited in text.
8. Annie Dillard, *An American Childhood* (New York: Harper and Row, 1987), 41; hereafter cited in text as *AAC*.
9. Charles Moritz, ed., *Current Biography Yearbook 1983* (New York: H. W. Wilson, 1984), 112; hereafter cited in text.
10. "Overlooking Glastonbury" appeared in *Transatlantic Review* (22 [Autumn 1966]:60) under Annie's maiden name, Annie Doak, on the same page with a poem by her husband. "The Affluent Beatnik" appeared in *The Girl in the Black Raincoat* ([New York: Duell, Sloan, and Pearce, 1966], 340). George Garrett was the editor of both the journal and the book.
11. R. H. W. Dillard, *After Borges* (Baton Rouge: Louisiana State University Press, 1972), 29.
12. R. H. W. Dillard, *News of the Nile* (Chapel Hill: University of North Carolina Press, 1971), 47.
13. Gail Caldwell, "Pilgrim's Progress," *Boston Globe Magazine*, 8 May 1983, 32; hereafter cited in text.
14. Paul S. Nathan, "A Writer Arrives," *Publishers Weekly*, 10 December 1973, 22.
15. Laurie Krauth, "Diving into Life with Annie Dillard," *Toledo Blade*, 14 February 1988, sec. F, 2; hereafter cited in text.
16. "A Writer's Desk," *Saturday Review*, May–June 1986, 23.
17. Alvin P. Sanoff, "Remembrances of Things Past," *U.S. World and News Report*, 16 November 1987, 78.

18. Andrea Chambers, "Annie Dillard: Her Pilgrimage This Time Is into Her Past," *People*, 19 October 1987, 105; hereafter cited in text.

Chapter Two

1. Alan Richardson and John Bowden, ed., *The Westminster Dictionary of Christian Theology* (Philadelphia: Westminster Press, 1983), 423; Walter A. Elwell, ed., *The Evangelical Dictionary of Theology* (Grand Rapids, Mich.: Baker Book House, 1984), 818–20. Richardson and Bowden hereafter cited in text.

2. Karla M. Hammond, "Drawing the Curtains: An Interview with Annie Dillard," *Bennington Review* 10 (April 1981):32; hereafter cited in text.

3. Gershom Scholem, *Kabbalah* (New York: Dorset Press, 1974), 128–44.

4. Paul Edwards, ed., *The Encyclopedia of Philosophy* (New York: Macmillan, 1967), 3:489–90; Titus Burckhardt, *Alchemy* (Worcester, England: Element Books, 1967). Burkhardt hereafter cited in text.

5. Annie Dillard, *Pilgrim at Tinker Creek* (New York: Harper's Magazine Press, 1974), 102; hereafter cited in text as *PTC*.

6. James N. Powell, *The Tao of Symbols* (New York: Quill, 1982), 141.

7. The *via creativa*, a phrase apparently coined by the contemporary theologian Matthew Fox, is discussed in great length in his *Original Blessing* (Santa Fe, N.M.: Bear, 1983). The general concept, however, is presented in Joseph Campbell's *The Masks of God: Creative Mythology* (New York: Penguin Books, 1968).

8. Michelle Murray, "Ms. Dillard: In Her Creek a Sense of How Things Are," *National Observer*, 23 March 1974, 27; *Choice,* September 1974, 921; hereafter cited in text.

9. Eudora Welty, "Meditation on Seeing," *New York Times Book Review*, 24 March 1974, 5; Margaret McFadden-Gerber, "The I in Nature," *American Notes and Queries* 16 (September 1977):4; Melvin Maddocks, "Terror and Celebration," *Time*, 18 March 1974, 92; Charles Nicol, "Looking Spring in the Eye," *National Review*, 26 April 1974, 489; Nancy Lucas, in *Dictionary of Literary Biography Yearbook: 1980*, ed. Karen L. Rood, Jean W. Ross, and Richard Ziegfeld (Detroit: Gale Research, 1981), 186.

10. McFadden-Gerber, 3; John C. Elder, "John Muir and the Literature of Wilderness," *Massachusetts Review* 22 (Summer 1981):375; Albert E. Stone, "Autobiography in American Culture: Looking back at the Seventies," *American Studies International* 19 (Spring–Summer 1981):2. Stone hereafter cited in text.

11. *Choice*, September 1974, 921.

12. Mary Davidson McConahay, "'Into the Bladelike Arms of God': The Quest for Meaning through Symbolic Language in Thoreau and Annie Dillard," *Denver Quarterly* 20 (Fall 1985):111, 115; hereafter cited in text.

13. Annie Dillard, "My New England Bookshelf," *New England Monthly*, November 1985, 67.

14. See, for example, Carol Christ's treatment in *Diving Deep and Surfacing: Women Writers on Spiritual Quest*, 2d ed. (Boston: Beacon Press, 1986).

15. Mircea Eliade, *The Sacred and the Profane*, trans. Willard R. Trask (San Diego, Calif.: Harcourt Brace Jovanovich, 1959).

16. Loren Eiseley, "Walden with Pizzazz," *Washington Post Book World*, 31 March 1974, 3.

17. Muriel Haynes, "We Are All Nibblers," *Ms.*, August 1974, 38.

18. Haynes, 38; Edmund Fuller, "Superb Insights of a Naturalist," *Wall Street Journal*, 26 June 1974, 18; Russell Hunt, "What You Get Is What You See," *Fiddlehead* 102 (Summer 1974):15; *Booklist*, 1 October 1977, 970.

19. John F. Baker, "Story behind the Book: *Pilgrim at Tinker Creek*," *Publishers Weekly*, 18 March 1974, 28.

Chapter Three

1. Leonard Randolph, "*Tickets for a Prayer Wheel*," *Living Wilderness* 38 (Summer 1974):37; *Choice*, July/August 1974, 757.

2. An illustration of this problem is reviewer Leonard Randolph's warning to his readers about the likely difficulty of obtaining a copy of Dillard's poems from a bookstore. He grumbled that "bookstores hate single-orders. And they don't like to stock poetry" (Randolph, 757).

3. Annie Dillard, *Teaching a Stone to Talk: Expeditions and Encounters* (New York: Harper and Row, 1982).

4. Charles Trueheart, "Annie Dillard: Pilgrim's Progress," *Washington Post*, 28 October 1987, sec. D, 3; hereafter cited in text.

5. Annie Dillard, "The Purification of Poetry—Right out of the Ballpark," *Parnassus* 11 (Fall/Winter–Spring/Summer 1984):287–301; hereafter cited in text as "Poetry."

6. Susan Chira, "Writers Impart Skills and Styles at Wesleyan," *New York Times*, 14 October 1983, sec. 2, 2.

7. Annie Dillard, "The Shape of Change: Idea in Theodore Roethke's Love Poetry," *Mill Mountain Review* 2 (1975):125–35.

8. Annie Dillard, *Tickets for a Prayer Wheel* (Columbia: University of Missouri Press, 1974); hereafter cited in text as *TPW*.

9. See Jan Susina, ed., *Poet as Zimmer, Zimmer as Poet* (Houston: Ford-Brown, 1986), which reprints Dillard's poem, along with several "Zimmer poems" written by other poets, in addition to a selection of Zimmer's own poems.

10. Karla M. Hammond, "Drawing the Curtains: An Interview with Annie Dillard," *Bennington Review* 10 (April 1981): 35.

11. Annie Dillard, comments in contributors' list in *Songs from Unsung Worlds: Science in Poetry*, ed. Bonnie Bilyeu Gordon, (Boston: Birkhauser, 1985), 214.

12. Annie Dillard, "Light in the Open Air," in Gordon, 87–89.

13. Annie Dillard, "Monarchs in the Field," *Harper's*, October 1976, 104.

14. Annie Dillard, "The Sign of Your Father," *Field* 11 (Autumn 1974): 23–24.

15. Annie Dillard, "Metaphysical Model with Feathers," *Atlantic*, October 1978, 82.

16. Annie Dillard, "Conifers," *Field* 11 (Autumn 1974): 25.

17. Annie Dillard, "Soft Coral," *Antigonish Review* 48 (1982):5.

Chapter Four

1. Annie Dillard, *Holy the Firm* (New York: Harper and Row, 1977), 24; hereafter cited in text as *HF.*

2. Frederick Buechner, "Island Journal," *New York Times Book Review*, 25 September 1988, 12, 40; hereafter cited in text.

3. Eugene H. Peterson, "Annie Dillard: Praying with Her Eyes Open," *Theological Students Fellowship Bulletin* 8 (January/February 1985):7–11.

4. Helen Hill Hitchcock, "Annie Dillard: Mystique of Nature," *Communio: International Catholic Review* 5 (Winter 1978):388–92.

5. Philip Yancey, "A Face Aflame: An Interview with Annie Dillard," *Christianity Today*, 5 May 1978, 958–63; hereafter cited in text.

6. Nancy Lucas, in *Dictionary of Literary Biography Yearbook: 1980*, ed. Karen L. Rood, Jean W. Ross, and Richard Ziegfeld (Detroit: Gale Research, 1981), 1987.

7. Annie Dillard, *The Writing Life* (New York: Harper and Row, 1989), 54.

8. Michael Burnett, "An Interview with Annie Dillard," *Fairhaven Review* (1978):96; hereafter cited in text.

9. Charles Trueheart, "Annie Dillard's Pilgrim's Progress," *Washington Post*, 28 October 1987, sec. D, 2; hereafter cited in text.

10. *Publisher's Weekly*, 1 August 1977, 109; Trueheart, 1; John Clifford, "Distinctive Nonfiction to Teach By," *English Journal* 68 (December 1979):73; Buechner, 40.

11. Thomas Cooley, preface, in *The Norton Sampler*, 3d ed., ed. Thomas Cooley (New York: W. W. Norton, 1985), xvii; Annie Dillard's "How I Wrote the Moth Essay—and Why," also in this volume, hereafter cited in text as "How I Wrote."

12. In "How I Wrote the Moth Essay—and Why" (p. 20) Dillard relates that when writing *Holy the Firm*, she owned a yellow cat whose name was actually Kindling. Deciding the truth was too incredible, she conflated the yellow cat Kindling with her black cat Small, resulting in the half-fictitious yellow cat Small.

13. Jacob C. Gaskins, "'Julie Norwich' and Julian of Norwich: Notes and a Query," *Fourteenth Century English Mystics Newsletter*, 1980, 153– 63.

14. J. C. J. Metford, *Dictionary of Christian Lore and Legend* (London: Thames and Hudson, 1983), 88.

15. John A. Miles, *Parabolas*, no. 2, (1978):112; Buechner, 12.

16. Mike Major, "Annie Dillard: Pilgrim of the Absolute," *America*, 6 May 1978, 363.

17. John Shea, *Critic: A Catholic Review of Books and the Arts* 34 (Summer 1978):76.

18. Karla M. Hammond, "Drawing the Curtains: An Interview with Annie Dillard," *Bennington Review* 10 (April 1981):33.

Chapter Five

1. Bruce A. Ronda, "Annie Dillard's Fictions to Live By," *Christian Century*, 14 November 1984, 1062–66.

2. Cathleen Medwick, "Beattie and Dillard: Writing to Save Their Lives," *Vogue*, October 1982, 84.

3. Philip Yancey, "A Face Aflame: An Interview with Annie Dillard," *Christianity Today*, 5 May 1978, 958–63.

4. Annie Dillard, *Teaching a Stone to Talk: Expeditions and Encounters* (New York: Harper and Row, 1982), 12; hereafter cited in text as *TST*.

5. Virginia Stem Owens, "Truth through Testimony: The Fierce Voice of Annie Dillard," *Reformed Journal* 33 (April 1983):23–25; hereafter cited in text.

6. Annie Dillard, "Postscript on Process," in *The Bedford Reader*, 2d ed., ed. J. Kennedy and Dorothy M. Kennedy (New York: St. Martin's Press, 1985), 110.

7. Carol Luebering, *St. Anthony Messenger* 91 (August 1983): 48; *Kirkus Reviews*, 1 August 1982, 913.

8. David S. Miller, "The Silence of Nature," *Sewanee Review* 92 (Winter 1984):161.

9. Medwick, "Beattie and Dillard," 84; David Lavery, review in *Religion and Literature* 17 (Summer 1985):62.

10. Christopher Lehmann-Haupt, "Books of the Times," *New York Times*, 21 September 1977, sec. C, 18.

Chapter Six

1. Jerome Klinkowitz, "Fiction: The 1950's to the Present," in *American Literary Scholarship: An Annual—1982*, ed. J. Albert Robbins (Durham, N.C.: Duke University Press, 1984), 272; David Sundelson, *Nation*, 20 November 1982, 535.

2. Kathryn Kilgore, "Metaphysics in a Teacup," *Village Voice*, 13 July 1982, 41.

3. Vance Bourjaily, "Contemporary Modernists—A Dreadful Mouthful," *New York Times Book Review*, 9 May 1982, 10; Janet Wiehe, *Library Journal*, 15 March 1982, 638; Andrea Barnet, *Saturday Review*, March 1982, 79; Kilgore, 41. Bourjaily hereafter cited in text.

4. Victor Howes, "Novelist Dillard Turns Literary Critic," *Christian Science Monitor*, 9 April 1982, sec. B, 6.

5. Annie Dillard, *Living by Fiction* (New York: Harper and Row, 1982), 11; hereafter cited in text as *LBF.*

6. Nancy Lucas, in *Dictionary of Literary Biography Yearbook: 1980,* ed. Karen L. Rood, Jean W. Ross, and Richard Ziegfeld (Detroit: Gale Research, 1981), 189.

7. F. Moramarco, *American Book Review* 5 (November 1982):8; hereafter cited in text.

8. John Breslin, "The Feel and Fabric of Fiction," *Washington Post World,* 4 April 1982, 4; hereafter cited in text.

9. Bill Ott, *Booklist,* 1 March 1982, 844.

10. Philip Yancey, "This Pulitzer Prize Winner Understands Both Christians and Skeptics," *Christianity Today,* 15 July 1983, 52.

11. W. H. New, *Canadian Literature* 102 (Autumn 1984):199.

12. Christopher Lehmann-Haupt, *New York Times,* 12 March 1982, sec. 3, 25.

13. Keith Cushman, *Studies in Short Fiction* 20 (Winter 1983):66.

14. K. McCormick Price, *San Diego Magazine,* May 1982, 102; hereafter cited in text.

15. See James Agee, "A Mother's Tale," The Collected Stories of James Agee (Boston: Houghton Mifflin Co., 1930), 221–43; Tommaso Landolfi, "Week of Sun," *Cancerqueen and Other Stories* (New York: Dial Press, 1971), 205–23; Italo Calvino, *Cosmicomics,* trans. William Weaver (New York: Harcourt Brace & World, 1968); and Philip Roth, *The Breast* (New York: Holt, Rinehart & Winston, 1972).

Chapter Seven

1. Annie Dillard, *Encounters with Chinese Writers* (New York: Harper and Row, 1984), 3; hereafter cited in text as *ECW.*

2. Ron Silver, *Saturday Review,* March/April 1985, 65.

3. Dinane Broughton, "Mission Inscrutable: Omission," *Los Angeles Times Book Review,* 18 November 1984, 11.

4. Dennis Drabelle, *Washington Post Book World,* 4 September 1984, 6; *Kirkus Reviews,* 15 July 1984, 670.

5. Jacqueline Eis, *Georgia Review* 39 (Winter 1985):906; hereafter cited in text.

Conclusion

1. Annie Dillard, ed., *The Best American Essays— 1988* (New York: Ticknor and Fields, 1988), xvii; hereafter cited in text as *Best Essays.*

2. Annie Dillard, *Teaching a Stone to Talk: Expeditions and Encounters* (New York: Harper and Row, 1982); hereafter cited in text as *TST.*

3. Annie Dillard, *An American Childhood* (New York: Harper and Row, 1989), 125; hereafter cited in text as *AAC*.

4. Annie Dillard, foreword to *Moments of Light*, by Fred Chappell (New York: New South, 1980), xiv; hereafter cited in text as "Foreword."

5. Annie Dillard, "My New England Bookshelf," *New England Monthly*, November 1985, 66.

6. Annie Dillard, "To Fashion a Text," in *Inventing the Truth: The Art and Craft of Memoir*, ed. William Zinsser (New York: Book-of-the-Month Club Press, 1987), 76.

7. Annie Dillard, *The Writing Life* (New York: Harper and Row, 1989), 78; hereafter cited in text as *WL*.

Selected Bibliography

PRIMARY WORKS

Books

An American Childhood. New York: Harper and Row, 1987. Paperback reprint edition, 1988.

The Best American Essays. Guest editor. New York: Ticknor and Fields, 1988.

Encounters with Chinese Writers. Middletown, Conn.: Wesleyan University Press, 1984. Paperback reprint edition, 1985.

Holy the Firm. New York: Harper and Row, 1977. Large print edition, G. K. Hall, 1978. Paperback reprint editions, Harper and Row, 1984, 1988.

Living by Fiction. New York: Harper and Row, 1982. Paperback reprint editions, Harper Colophon Books, 1983, 1988.

Pilgrim at Tinker Creek. New York: Harper's Magazine Press, 1974. Paperback reprint edition, Bantam Books, 1975. London hardback edition, Jonathan Cape, 1975. London paperback edition, Pan Books, 1976. Paperback reprint editions, Harper and Row, Perennial Library edition, 1985, 1988.

Teaching a Stone to Talk: Expeditions and Encounters. New York: Harper and Row, 1982. Paperback reprint editions, Harper and Row, 1983, 1988. London paperback edition, Pan Books, 1984.

Tickets for a Prayer Wheel. Columbia: University of Missouri Press, 1974. Paperback reprint edition, Bantam Books, 1975. Paperback reprint edition, Harper and Row, 1986.

The Weasel. Claremont, Calif.: Rara Avis Press, 1981. Limited edition of 190 copies.

The Writing Life. New York: Harper and Row, 1989. Paperback reprint edition, 1990.

Essays

"Artists of the Beautiful." *Living Wilderness*, Winter 1974–75, 62–63. Reprinted in a slightly different form in *Teaching a Stone to Talk.*

"The Bats." *Hollins* 32 (Spring 1982):11.

"Birdsong." *Living Wilderness*, Spring 1974, 2–3. Reprinted in slightly different form as chapter 2 of *Pilgrim at Tinker Creek.*

"Blue Ridge Spring." *Prose* 8 (Spring 1974):73–91. Reprinted in a slightly different form as chapter 2 of *Pilgrim at Tinker Creek.*

"Catching the Season." *Living Wilderness*, Winter 1973–74, 2–3. Reprinted as chapter 3 of *Pilgrim at Tinker Creek*.

"Contemporary Prose Styles." *Twentieth Century Literature* 27 (Fall 1981):207–22. Reprinted as chapter 7 of *Living by Fiction*.

"The Death of a Moth." *Harper's*, May 1976, 26–27. Reprinted in revised form as part 1 of *Holy the Firm*.

"The Deer at Providencia." *Living Wilderness*, Spring 1975, 46–47. Reprinted in *Teaching a Stone to Talk*.

"An Expedition to the Pole." *Yale Literary Magazine* 150 (June 1982):37–57. Reprinted with minor changes in *Teaching a Stone to Talk*.

"A Field of Silence." *Atlantic*, February 1978, 74–76. Reprinted in *Teaching a Stone to Talk*.

"Footfalls in a Blue Ridge Winter." *Sports Illustrated*, February 1974, 72–76, 79–80. Reprinted in a slightly different form as part of chapter 3 of *Pilgrim at Tinker Creek*.

"For the Love of China." *Harvard Magazine*, July–August 1983, 38–44. Reprinted in revised form in *Encounters with Chinese Writers*.

"The Force That Drives the Flower." *Atlantic*, November 1973, 69– 72, 74–77. Reprinted with minor changes as chapter 10 of *Pilgrim at Tinker Creek*.

"The French and Indian War in Pittsburgh: A Memoir." *American Heritage*, July–August 1987, 49–53.

"Heaven and Earth in Jest." *Harper's*, October 1973, 73–74. Reprinted in a slightly different form in *Pilgrim at Tinker Creek*.

"How I Wrote the Moth Essay—and Why." In *The Norton Sampler*, edited by Thomas Cooley, 13–21. New York: W. W. Norton, 1985.

"Innocence in the Galapagos." *Harper's*, May 1975, 74, 77–82. Reprinted in a slightly revised form as "Life on the Rocks" in *Teaching a Stone to Talk*.

"Is Art All There Is?" *Harper's* August 1980, 61–66. Reprinted as part of chapter 1 and most of chapter 3 of *Living by Fiction*.

"Is There Really Such a Thing as Talent?" *Seventeen*, June 1979, 86. Reprinted in *The Elements of Writing*, edited by Peter D. Lindblom. New York: Macmillan, 1983, 154–56.

"The Joys of Reading." *New York Times Magazine*, 16 May 1982, 47, 68–69, 78–81.

"Jungle Peace." *Holiday*, September–October 1975, 24–27, 52. Reprinted in a slightly revised form as "In the Jungle" in *Teaching a Stone to Talk*.

"Learning to Chop Wood." *Christian Science Monitor*, 24 January 1979, 2. Incorporated into "Wish I Had Pie" and later into *The Writing Life*.

"The Leg in the Christmas Stocking: What We Learned from Jokes." *New York Times Book Review*, 7 December 1986, 51. Incorporated into *The Writing Life*.

"Making Contact." *Yale Review* 72 (October 1988):615–22.

"Mirages." *Harper's*, December 1977, 84–85. Reprinted in a slightly different form in *Teaching a Stone to Talk*.

"Monster in a Mason Jar." *Harper's*, August 1973, 61–64, 66–67. Reprinted as part of chapter 3 of *Pilgrim at Tinker Creek*.

"My New England Bookshelf." *New England Monthly*, November 1985, 66–68.

"A Note on Process." *Christian Science Monitor*, 30 April 1979, 25. Incorporated into "Wish I Had Pie."

"A Note on Process." *Jeopardy* 15 (Spring 1979):8.

"On a Hill Far Away." *Harper's*, October 1975, 22, 24–25. Reprinted in revised form in *Teaching a Stone to Talk*.

"Postscript on Process." In *The Bedford Reader*, edited by X. J. Kennedy and Dorothy M. Kennedy, 107–11. New York: St. Martin's Press, 1985.

"The Purification of Poetry—Right out of the Ballpark." *Parnassus* 11 (1984): 287–301.

"Reflections on an Island." *Science*, April 1981, 62–67.

"The Shape of Change: Idea in Theodore Roethke's Love Poetry." *Mill Mountain Review* 2(1975):125–35.

"Sight into Insight." *Harper's*, February 1974, 39–40, 42, 44–46. Reprinted in revised form in *Pilgrim at Tinker Creek*.

"Singing with the Fundamentalists." *Yale Review* 74 (Winter 1985):312–20.

"Sojourner." *Living Wilderness*, Autumn 1973, 2–3. Partially incorporated into "The Present" in *Pilgrim at Tinker Creek*.

"Sojourner." *Living Wilderness*, Summer 1974, 2–3. Reprinted as "Living Like Weasels" in *Teaching a Stone to Talk*.

"Some Notes on the Uncertainty Principle." *New Lazarus Review* 1 (1978):49–50.

"A Speech on Socks." *New York Times*, 12 December 1978, sec. A, 23.

"The State of the Art—Fiction and Its Audience." *Massachusetts Review* 23 (Spring 1982):85–96. Reprinted in revised form as chapter 5 of *Living by Fiction*.

"Streetcars." In *Our Roots Grow Deeper Than We Know*, edited by Lee Gutkind, 45–47. Pittsburgh: University of Pittsburgh Press, 1985. Reprinted in *An American Childhood*.

"Teaching a Stone to Talk." *Atlantic*, February 1981, 36–39. Reprinted in *Teaching a Stone to Talk*.

"Thinking about Language." *Living Wilderness* (Autumn 1974):2–3.

"To Fashion a Text." In *Inventing the Truth: The Art and Craft of Memoir*, edited by William Zinsser, 53–76. New York: Book-of-the-Month Club Press, 1987.

"Total Eclipse." *Antaeus* (Spring–Summer 1982):43–55. Reprinted with minor changes in *Teaching a Stone to Talk*.

"Transfiguration." In *The Norton Sampler*, edited by Thomas Cooley, 7–10. New York: W. W. Norton, 1985. Reprinted in revised form in *Holy the Firm*.

"A Watcher of Things." *Christian Science Monitor*, 8 April 1982, 20. Reprinted as "Lenses" in *Teaching a Stone to Talk*.

"Why I Live Where I Live." *Esquire*, March 1984, 90–92.

"Winter Melons." *Harper's*, January 1974, 87, 89–90.

"Wish I Had Pie." *Black Warrior Review* 8 (Spring 1982):75–84. Reprinted in revised form in *The Writing Life*.

"With the Chinese at Disneyland." *Harper's*, September 1984, 21–22. Reprinted in *Encounters with Chinese Writers*.

"Write Till You Drop." *New York Times Book Review*, 28 May 1989, sec. 7, 1, 23. Reprinted in *The Writing Life*.

"Writing 'God in the Doorway.'" In *Writing from Start to Finish*, edited by Jeffrey L. Duncan, 279–83. New York: Harcourt Brace, 1985.

Poetry

"The Affluent Beatnik." In *The Girl in the Black Raincoat*, edited by George Garrett, 340. New York: Duell, Sloan, and Pearce, 1966.

"After Noon." *Carolina Quarterly* 15 (Fall 1973):60. Reprinted in a slightly different form in *Tickets for a Prayer Wheel*.

"The Blind Spot." *Concerning Poetry* 9, no. 1 (1976):4.

"Christmas." *Hollins Critic* 6 (December 1969):11. Reprinted in a slightly different form in *Tickets for a Prayer Wheel*.

"Conifers." *Field* 11 (Autumn 1974): 25.

"The Dominion of Trees." *Carolina Quarterly* 23 (Fall 1971):76–77. Reprinted in a slightly different form in *Tickets for a Prayer Wheel*.

"Eleanor at the Office." *New York Quarterly* 9 (Winter 1972):80. Reprinted in a slightly different form in *Tickets for a Prayer Wheel*.

"Eskimos." *Southern Poetry Review* 14, no. 1 (Spring 1974):66. Reprinted in a slightly different form in *Tickets for a Prayer Wheel*.

"Farmer's Daughter." *Contempora* 1, no. 6 (May–August 1971):49. Reprinted in a slightly different form in *Tickets for a Prayer Wheel*.

"Feast Days." *Atlantic*, December 1973, 67. Reprinted in a slightly different form in *Tickets for a Prayer Wheel*.

"The Heart." *Poetry* 125 (February 1975):260.

"Language for Everyone." *Southwest Review* 71 (1986):488–92.

"Light in the Open Air." In *Songs from Unsung Worlds: Science in Poetry*, edited by Bonnie B. Gordon, 87–89. Boston: Birkhauser, 1985.

"The Man Who Wishes to Feed on Mahogany." *American Scholar* 42, no. 2 (Spring 1973):279–80. Reprinted in *Tickets for a Prayer Wheel*.

"Metaphysical Model with Feathers." *Atlantic*, October 1978, 82.

"Monarchs in the Field." *Harper's*, October 1976, 104.

"A Natural History of Getting through the Year." *Poetry* 125 (February 1975): 261.

"Overlooking Glastonbury." *Transatlantic Review* 22 (Autumn 1966):60. Reprinted in a slightly different form in *Tickets for a Prayer Wheel*.

"Quatrain of the Body's Sleep." *Poetry* 125 (February 1975):262.

"The Sign of Your Father." *Field* 11 (Autumn 1974):23–24.

"Soft Coral." *Antigonish Review* 48 (1982):5.

"Tying His Tie and Whistling a Tune, Zimmer Strikes a Nostalgic Note and Invents His Past." *Contempora* 2, no. 2 (March–July 1972):33. Reprinted in a slightly different form in *Tickets for a Prayer Wheel.* Also reprinted in *Poet as Zimmer, Zimmer as Poet,* edited by Jan Susina, 101. Houston: Ford-Brown, 1986.

"The Weighing of Daleville." *New Orleans Review* 4 (1974):204.

"The Windy Planet." In *Songs from Unsung Worlds: Science in Poetry,* edited by Bonnie B. Gordon, 87–89. Boston: Birkhauser, 1985.

Short Stories

"At Home with Gastropods—A Nineteenth Century Interior, in Translation." *North American Review* 263 (Spring 1978):50.

"A Christmas Story." *Harper's,* January 1976, 58.

"The Doughnut." *Antioch Review* 34 (Fall–Winter 1975–76):22– 25.

"Ethiopian Monastery." *Hollins Critic* 10 (August 1973):12.

"Five Sketches." *North American Review* 260 (Summer 1975):30–31.

"Forest and Shore." *Harper's,* January 1985, 24.

"Four Bits." *Ploughshares* 10, no. 2–3 (1984):68–73. Reprinted from "Five Sketches" in *North American Review.*

"Life Class." *Carolina Quarterly* 24 (Spring 1972):23–27. Expanded and revised version reprinted in *Antaeus* 36 (Winter 1980):52–60.

"The Living." *Harper's,* November 1978, 45–52, 57–64.

"The Stone." *Chicago Review* 26, no. 4 (1975):152–53.

"Stone Doctor." *Epoch* 26 (Fall 1976):63.

"Utah." *TriQuarterly* 35 (Spring 1976):96–98.

Miscellaneous

"Critics' Christmas Choices." *Commonweal,* 7 December 1979, 693–94.

"First Taste of America." *American Heritage,* December 1984, 26.

Foreword to *Moments of Light,* by Fred Chappell, ix–xvii. New York: New South, 1980.

Foreword to *Wind on the Sand: The Hidden Life of an Anchoress,* v–vi. Ramsey, N.J.: Paulist Press, 1981.

"The Good Books: Writers' Choices." Edited by Karen Fitzgerald. *Ms.,* December 1985, 80–81.

"John Moore: A Sense of Proportion, a Gracious Heart." *Hollins Magazine,* October 1985, 8–9.

"The Meaning of Life." *Life,* December 1988, 93.

"Memories of the Season." *Pittsburgh Magazine,* December 1985, 38.

"Natural History: An Annotated Booklist." *Antaeus,* no. 57 (1986):283–89.

"Reading for Work and Pleasure." *New York Times Book Review,* 4 December 1983, 66.

"Studied Composition." In *Bred Any Good Rooks Lately?* edited by James Charlton, 69. Garden City, N.Y.: Doubleday, 1986.

"Taking Another Look at the Constitutional Blueprint." *American Heritage,* May–June 1987, 67.

"Tales of Grandeur, Tales of Risk." *Harper's,* November 1974, 122.

"Walden Pond and Thoreau." Unpublished master's thesis, Hollins College, 1968.

SECONDARY WORKS

Articles and Book Chapters

Anhorn, Judy Schaaf. "Annie Dillard's 'Purified Nonfiction Narration.'" In *Cross-Cultural Studies: American, Canadian and European Literature 1945–1985,* edited by Mirko Jurak, 141–49. Ljubljana, Yugoslavia: Filozofska Fakulteta, 1988. Examines Dillard's use of multiple lines of narration as an outgrowth of natural history writing.

Baker, John F. "Story behind the Book: *Pilgrim at Tinker Creek.*" *Publisher's Weekly,* 18 March 1974, 28.

Becker, John E. "Science and the Sacred: From Walden to Tinker Creek." *Thought—A Review of Culture and Idea* 62, no. 247 (1987):400–13. Shows how *Walden* and *Pilgrim at Tinker Creek* convey a sense of sacred presence.

Dunn, Robert Paul. "The Artist as Nun: Theme, Tones, and Vision in the Writings of Annie Dillard." *Studia Mystica* 1 (Winter 1978):17–31. Discusses how Dillard uses images of artists, nuns, and anchorites as strategies of tone.

Elder, John. *Imagining the Earth: Poetry and the Vision of Nature.* Urbana: University of Illinois Press, 1985. Chapter 7, "Structures of Evolving Consciousness," 161–84, discusses *Pilgrim at Tinker Creek* and Peter Matthiessen's *Snow Leopard* as examples of Whitehead's "feeling approach" to the physical world.

Gaskins, Jacob C. "'Julie Norwich' and Julian of Norwich: Notes and a Query." *Fourteenth Century English Mystics Newsletter,* 1980, 153–63. Suggests allusions in *Holy the Firm* to the writing of the medieval mystic Julian of Norwich.

Keller, Joseph. "The Function of Paradox in Mystical Discourse." *Studia Mystica* 6 (Fall 1983):3–19. Treats the way Dillard uses paradox to simulate a nonanalysis of mystical experience.

Koenig, Rhoda. "About This Issue." *Harper's,* February 1974, 14.

Lavery, David L. "Noticer: The Visionary Art of Annie Dillard." *Massachusetts*

Review 21 (Summer 1980):255–70. Discusses how Dillard achieves a vision of monistic unity in *Pilgrim at Tinker Creek.*

Lucas, Nancy. "Annie Dillard." In *Dictionary of Literary Biography Yearbook: 1980,* edited by Karen L. Rood, Jean W. Ross, and Richard Ziegfeld, 184–89. Detroit: Gale Research, 1981.

McConahay, Mary Davidson. "Into the Bladelike Arms of God: The Quest for Meaning through Symbolic Language in Thoreau and Annie Dillard." *Denver Quarterly* 20 (Fall 1985):103–16. Describes Thoreau's and Dillard's use of symbolism to extend the capacity of language.

McFadden-Gerber, Margaret. "The I in Nature." *American Notes and Queries* 16 (September 1977):3–5. Debates the genre of *Pilgrim at Tinker Creek,* citing its "autobiographical center of gravity."

McIlroy, Gary. "Pilgrim at Tinker Creek and the Burden of Science." *American Literature: A Journal of Literature, History, Criticism, and Bibliography* 59, no. 1 (March 1987):71–84. Discusses Dillard's use of science in *Pilgrim at Tinker Creek.*

―――. "Pilgrim at Tinker Creek and the Social Legacy of Walden." *South Atlantic Quarterly* 85, no. 2 (Spring 1986):111–22. Describes Dillard's treatment of society and the individual in *Pilgrim at Tinker Creek.*

Messer, Richard E. "The Spiritual Quest in Two Works by Annie Dillard." *Journal of Evolutionary Psychology* 9, no. 3–4 (August 1988):321–30. Discusses *Pilgrim at Tinker Creek* and *Holy the Firm* as spiritual autobiography.

Nathan, Paul S. "A Writer Arrives." *Publisher's Weekly,* 10 December 1973, 22.

Owens, Virginia Stem. "Truth through Testimony: The Fierce Voice of Annie Dillard." *Reformed Journal* 33 (April 1983):23–25. Addresses how Dillard's work crosses genres and develops a new brand of storytelling.

Peterson, Eugene H. "Annie Dillard: Praying with her Eyes Open." *TSF Bulletin* 8 (January–February 1985):7–11. Compares Dillard's works to acts of worship and prayer.

Reimer, Margaret Loewen. "The Dialectical Vision of Annie Dillard's *Pilgrim at Tinker Creek.*" *Critique: Studies in Modern Fiction* 24 (Spring 1983):182–91. Compares with Melville's work the dialectical tension between beauty and horror in *Pilgrim at Tinker Creek.*

Ronda, Bruce A. "Annie Dillard and the Fire of God." *Christian Century* 100 (18 May 1983):483–86. Discusses Dillard's view of the role of suffering in spiritual growth.

―――. "Annie Dillard's Fictions to Live By." *Christian Century,* 14 November 1984, 1062–66. Examines how social commitment and engagement avoid the danger of subjectivism in Dillard's work.

Scheick, William J. "Annie Dillard—Narrative Fringe." In *Contemporary American Women Writers: Narrative Strategies,* edited by Catherine Rainwater and William J. Scheick, 50–67. Lexington: University Press of Kentucky, 1985.

Shows how Dillard's narrative technique parallels her concept of the point where time and eternity meet.

Ward, Patricia. "Annie Dillard's Way of Seeing." *Christianity Today,* 5 May 1978, 974–75. Examines Dillard's use of romantic and mystic traditions.

Wymard, Eleanor B. "A New Existential Voice." *Commonweal,* 24 October 1975, 495–96. Discusses Dillard's Christian response to existential realities in *Pilgrim.*

Yancey, Philip. "This Pulitzer Prize Winner Understands Both Christians and Skeptics." *Christianity Today,* 15 July 1983, 50, 52. Finds Dillard's work consistent with and sympathetic to the Christian fundamentalist movement.

Interviews

Burnett, Michael. "An Interview with Annie Dillard." *Fairhaven Review* (1978):87–102.

Caldwell, Gail. "Pilgrim's Progress." *Boston Globe Magazine,* 8 May 1983, 10–11, 32–37, 42, 48.

Chambers, Andrea. "Annie Dillard: Her Pilgrimage This Time Is into Her Past." *People,* 19 October 1987, 99–100, 105.

Hammond, Karla M. "Drawing the Curtains: An Interview with Annie Dillard." *Bennington Review* 10 (April 1981):30–38.

Krauth, Laurie. "Diving into Life with Annie Dillard." *Toledo Blade,* 14 February 1988, sec. F, 1–2.

Lindsey, Robert. "Annie Dillard, Far from Tinker Creek." *New York Times,* 9 November 1977, sec. C, 1, 7.

Major, Mike. "Annie Dillard: Pilgrim of the Absolute." *American* 138 (6 May 1978):363–64.

Sanoff, Alvin P. "Remembrances of Things Past." *U.S. News and World Reports,* 16 November 1987, 78.

Trueheart, Charles. "Annie Dillard's Pilgrim's Progress." *Washington Post,* 28 October 1987, sec. D, 1–3.

Yancey, Philip. "A Face Aflame: An Interview with Annie Dillard." *Christianity Today,* 5 May 1978, 958–63.

Book Reviews

Pilgrim at Tinker Creek (1974)

Breslin, John B. *"Pilgrim at Tinker Creek and Tickets for a Prayer Wheel."* *America* 130 (20 April 1974):312–14.

Buckner, Sally. *"Pilgrim at Tinker Creek."* In *Survey of Contemporary Literature,* edited by Frank N. Magill rev. ed., Englewood Cliffs, N.J.: Salem Press, 1977, vol 9, 5861–64.

Carruth, Hayden. "Attractions and Dangers of Nostalgia." *Virginia Quarterly Review* 50 (Autumn 1974):637–40.

Cunningham, Lawrence S. "Revisiting Tinker Creek." *Christian Century* 92 (3 September 1975):768–69.

Deemer, Charles. "Up the Creek." *New Leader* 57 (24 June 1974):18–20.

Eiseley, Loren. "Walden with Pizzazz." *Washington Post Book World*, 31 March 1974, 3.

Elder, Jeane. "Valley High, Island Low: The Natural Worlds of Annie Dillard and Josephine Johnson." *Snowy Egret* 39 (Spring 1976):28–31.

Haynes, Muriel. "We Are All Nibblers." *Ms.*, August 1974, 38–39.

Hoffman, Eva. "Solitude." *Commentary* 58 (October 1974):87–88, 90–91.

Hunt, Russell. "What You See Is What You See." *Fiddlehead* 102 (Summer 1974):113–19.

Kiser, Jo Ann. "*Pilgrim at Tinker Creek.*" *Village Voice*, 2 May 1974, 50–51.

Lehmann-Haupt, Christopher. "The Bloody Veil of Nature." *New York Times*, 12 March 1974, 35.

Maddocks, Melvin. "Terror and Celebration." *Time*, 18 March 1974, 92.

Murray, Michelle. "Ms. Dillard: In Her Creek a Sense of How Things Are." *National Observer*, 23 March 1974, 27.

Nicol, Charles. "Looking Spring in the Eye." *National Review*, 26 April 1974, 489.

Parker, Dorothy L. "Nature under a Poet's Laser-Gaze." *Christian Science Monitor*, 3 April 1974, sec. F, 4.

Peirce, J. C. "*Pilgrim at Tinker Creek.*" *Dalhousie Review* 54 (Autumn 1974):568–70.

Reisinger, Joyce. "*Pilgrim at Tinker Creek.*" *Cross Currents* 24 (Spring 1974): 119–21.

Welty, Eudora. "Meditation on Seeing." *New York Times Book Review*, 24 March 1974, 4.

Tickets for a Prayer Wheel (1974)

Randolph, Leonard. "*Tickets for a Prayer Wheel.*" *Living Wilderness*, Summer 1974, 37.

Holy the Firm (1977)

Beckwith, Barbara. *St. Anthony Messenger* 85 (November 1977):48–50.

Blake, Richard A. "Sacred and Profane: Fact, Fiction and Downright Fable." *America*, 8 October 1977, 219–20.

Buechner, Frederick. "Island Journal." *New York Times Book Review*, 25 September 1977, 12, 40.

Knudsen, Chilton. "*Holy the Firm.*" *Anglican Theological Review* 60 (October 1978):511–12.

Lemontt, Bobbie Burch. "*Holy the Firm.*" *Western American Literature* 13 (November 1978):274.

Miles, John A. "*Holy the Firm.*" *Parabola* 3, no. 2 (1978):111–14.

Phillips, Robert. "In Brief." *Commonweal*, 3 February 1978, 94.

Teaching a Stone to Talk (1982)

Bauer, Douglas. "Annie Dillard at Play in the Fields of the Lord." *Washington Post Book World*, 2 January 1983, 6.

Bevington, Helen. "Tranquil and Trembling." *New York Times Book Review*, 28 November 1982, 13, 19.

Breslin, John B. "*Teaching a Stone to Talk.*" *America*, 4 December 1982, 355–56.

Despot, Maggi. "Where the World Laps at Our Feet." *Sojourners*, May 1983, 42–43.

Hancock, Wade. "Transmuting the Invisible into Prose." *Christian Science Monitor*, 5 November 1982, sec. B, 3.

Lehmann-Haupt, Christopher. "Books of the Times." *New York Times*, 21 September 1977, sec. C, 17.

Luebering, Carol. "*Teaching a Stone to Talk.*" *St. Anthony Messenger* 91 (August 1983):48.

Smith, Huston. *Commonweal*, 3 December 1982, 668–69.

Smith, Marion. "*Teaching a Stone to Talk.*" *Epiphany* 4 (Winter 1983):113–15.

Living by Fiction (1982)

Bourjaily, Vance. "Contemporary Modernists—A Dreadful Mouthful." *New York Times Book Review*, 9 May 1982, 10, 22–23.

Breslin, John. "The Feel and Fabric of Fiction." *Washington Post Book World*, 4 April 1982, 4.

Kilgore, Kathryn. "Metaphysics in a Teacup." *Village Voice*, 13 July 1982, 40–41.

Moramarco, Fred. "*Living by Fiction.*" *American Book Review* 8 (November 1982):8.

Lavery, David. "*Living with Fiction, Teaching a Stone to Talk,* and *Encounters with Chinese Writers.*" *Religion and Literature* 17 (Summer 1985):61–68.

Sundelson, David. "Matthew Arnold She's Not." *Nation*, 20 November 1982, 535–36.

Encounters with Chinese Writers (1984)

Broughton, Diane. "Mission Inscrutable: Omission." *Los Angeles Times Book Review*, 18 November 1984, 11.

Eis, Jacqueline. "*Encounters with Chinese Writers.*" *Georgia Review* 39 (Winter 1985):906–7.

Herbert, Rosemary. "University Presses." *Christian Science Monitor Book Review*, 7 December 1984, sec. B, 14.

Silver, Ron. "*Encounters with Chinese Writers*." *Saturday Review*, March–April 1985, 64–65.

An American Childhood (1987)

Hazo, Samuel. "Attention Must Be Paid." *Commonweal*, 6 November 1987, 636–38.

Manuel, Diane. "From Dillard: A More Tolerant, Childlike Voice." *Christian Science Monitor*, 28 January 1988, 20.

Perrin, Noel. "Her Inexhaustible Mind." *New York Times Book Review*, 27 September 1987, 7.

Swartley, Ariel. "The Coming of Age of Annie Dillard." *Ms.*, 16 October 1987, 78, 80.

Index

The Author

Linda L. Smith earned her B.A. in English literature from Ohio State University in 1971 and a law degree from the University of Toledo in 1975. She now teaches in the English Department at the University of Toledo and conducts communications training for businesses. She is at present completing her doctoral work in English literature at the University of Toledo, as well as teaching courses in spiritual development at the Chiara Center at Lourdes College in Sylvania, Ohio.

The Editor

Frank Day is a professor of English at Clemson University. He is the author of *Sir William Empson: An Annotated Bibliography* and *Arthur Koestler: A Guide to Research*. He was a Fulbright Lecturer in American Literature in Romania (1980–81) and in Bangladesh (1986–87).